THE
AVERAGE FAMILY'S
GUIDE TO
FINANCIAL FREEDOM

BILL & MARY TOOHEY

JOHN WILEY & SONS, INC.

New York • Chichester • Weinheim
Brisbane • Singapore • Toronto

This book is printed on acid-free paper.

Copyright © 2000 by Bill Toohey and Mary Toohey. All rights reserved.

Published by John Wiley & Sons, Inc.

Published simultaneously in Canada.

No part of this publication may be reproduced, stored in a retrieval system or transmitted in any form or by any means, electronic, mechanical, photocopying, recording, scanning or otherwise, except as permitted under Section 107 or 108 of the 1976 United States Copyright Act, without either the prior written permission of the Publisher, or authorization through payment of the appropriate per-copy fee to the Copyright Clearance Center, 222 Rosewood Drive, Danvers, MA 01923, (978) 750-8400, fax (978) 750-4744. Requests to the Publisher for permission should be addressed to the Permissions Department, John Wiley & Sons, Inc., 605 Third Avenue, New York, NY 10158-0012, (212) 850-6011, fax (212) 850-6008, E-Mail: PERMREQ @ WILEY.COM.

Library of Congress Cataloging-in-Publication Data:

Toohey, Bill, 1952–
    The average family's guide to financial freedom / Bill Toohey and Mary Toohey.
        p. cm.
    Includes bibliographical references.
    ISBN 0-471-41627-4   (cloth : alk. paper)
    1. Family.   2. Finance, Personal.   I. Title.   II. Toohey, Mary, 1953–
HQ518.T58   2000
332.024 21—dc21   99-046190

10 9 8 7 6 5 4 3 2 1

To Lucilda Sewald, Derry and Jackie Jacobs, and Don Oviatt,
four heroes to whom we owe our deepest gratitude

ACKNOWLEDGMENTS

Thanks to Debby Englander, Olga Moya, Gowri Ramachandran, Mary Daniello, and the entire team at John Wiley & Sons for their tremendous professionalism, hard work, and support throughout this project.

Thanks also to Bernice Pettinato and all the staff of Beehive Production Services for working tirelessly to make this book better.

Special thanks to Malaga Baldi, an outstanding literary agent who guided us through the publication process with remarkable kindness, skill, and professionalism.

BILL AND MARY TOOHEY

CONTENTS

Introduction   1

PART ONE
BUILDING A MONEY-SAVING MINDSET
11

Love: The Impact of Money on Relationships   13

Crisis: Maintaining Normalcy in a Crisis   16

Comfort: How to Be Comfortable in a Modest Home   19

Study: How Learning Contributes to Peace, Order,
   and Financial Freedom   22

Gratitude: Grandma's Red Brick House and Why We Need
   to Have an "Attitude of Gratitude"   25

PART TWO
SPENDING LESS IS EASIER THAN SAVING MORE
29

Saving: Why Saving Doesn't Work   31

Spending: The Double Whammy of Spending Control   34

Categorize: Categorize Your Spending and Zero In
   on Problem Areas   36

Contents

Surprise: Avoiding the Trap of Failing to Plan for All Expenses   40

Borrowing: Despising Debt   44

Creep: The Perils of Increasing Your Standard of Living
Too Quickly   50

PART THREE
NECESSITIES AND A FEW EXTRAS
53

Home: Choosing the Right House Will Make You or Break You   55

Wheels: Car-Buying Secrets   59

Supermarket: How a College Class Assignment
Changed Our Approach to Grocery Shopping   67

Entertainment: Having Fun Without Breaking the Bank   70

Impulse: How to Control Miscellaneous Spending   73

Splurge: Coming Up for Air   78

PART FOUR
BIG TICKET MONEY SAVERS
81

Research: Money-Saving Strategies for Big Ticket Purchases   83

Scholarship: A Debt-Free College Education for $7000!   88

Taxes: Taking Advantage of Tax Breaks   91

PART FIVE
SIMPLIFY YOUR LIFE
97

Supplies: Office Supplies You Must Have   99

Files: Building a Bulletproof Filing System   103

Contents

Bathroom: Strategies That Keep a One Bathroom Home
Running Smoothly   107

Sleep: The Costs of Losing Sleep   110

PART SIX
PRACTICAL MONEY-SAVING SKILLS
115

Refunds: Recouping Your Money on Shoddy Work, Products,
or Insurance Denials   117

Maintenance: Make Your Things Last Forever   122

Skills: Do It Yourself and Save   126

Commissions: Avoiding Sales Commissions and Insurance
Company Financial Products   132

PART SEVEN
BE YOUR OWN FINANCIAL EXPERT
137

Planners: The Best Financial Planner for You Is You   139

Foundation: Building Your Financial Future on Solid Footing   142

Homework: Investing Knowledge . . . Where to Get It   146

PART EIGHT
INVESTING
155

Stocks: Breaking Through the Minimum Wage Mentality   157

Bonds: Smoothing Out the Dips   163

Cash: A Risky Investment   168

Allocation: Asset Allocation—The Family's Most Important
Investment Decision   171

Contents

Funds: No-Load Mutual Funds—The Way Families
  Should Invest   177

Choosing: Drowning in a Sea of Choices   180

When: When to Buy, When to Sell, When to Adjust   185

Dumb Moves: Our Investment Mistakes   190

PART NINE
RETIREMENT
195

Plans: IRAs, Roths, 403(b)s, 401(k)s, SIMPLES, SEPs, Keoghs . . .   197

Withdrawing: Getting Your Money Out of Retirement
  Plans Whenever You Want—Without Penalties   204

Enough: Keeping Our Money from Petering Out Before We Do   207

Threats: A Sample of Things That Can Go Wrong   212

PART TEN
PARENTING
217

Supper: We Raise Our Kids at Dinner   219

Indulge: Spending Money on Kids   222

Discipline: Chaos Poses a Threat to Your Family's
  Financial Health   226

Expectations: Setting High Expectations for Children
  Without Driving Them Crazy   230

Teens: Getting Through the Tough Years Without Losing
  Your Money or Your Mind   235

Afterword   239

Index   241

INTRODUCTION

Winter 1991. My wife and I are in our late thirties. We have a daughter about to finish high school, a son with severe disabilities and health problems, and a daughter in elementary school. Our total income is only a little more than $34,000. We have a mortgage, car payments, and huge college bills looming ahead. Most of our small $63,000 savings is tied up in our home equity and in a retirement plan at work. The economy is in the tank and my job is at risk.

Winter 1999. Our daughter has a college degree that is completely paid for, we own our home and two cars, free and clear, and the value of our assets is $467,000.

Hi. I'm Bill Toohey. My wife, Mary, and I are just average people, working regular jobs, earning modest incomes. We love our family, have great friends, and enjoy our low-key lives. We've never intended to achieve fame, build a fortune, or earn big bucks. Like most Americans, our interests have led us into careers that don't pay a lot. We're not exactly poor, but we've always been closer to poor than to rich. In fact, I've never broken through $40,000 at my job and Mary has only recently topped $20,000 at hers.

I'm a state vocational rehabilitation counselor. If you have a disability and you are looking for help to enter the workforce, I'm the guy you come to. I've been doing that for about 23 years. Mary has been managing a small professional office for more than 20 years. We don't earn big salaries and, like most people, we never will. But hey, many of us don't want to be attorneys, physicians, administrators, and business owners. We're drawn to other things, and that's good, because we need teachers, police officers, farmers, social workers, nurses, carpenters, secretaries, retail clerks, and meat cutters. Most of us are doing what we want, what we're cut out to do. We're living the lives we choose. We go to work, do our jobs as best we can, and look forward to weekends. Life is good. But there are economic trends that pose threats to families like ours and probably pose hazards for your family, too.

Companies are downsizing and employees who keep their jobs are burning out from trying to keep up with more work and fewer people to do it. Pressure to be totally productive is intense. Factory lines are speeding up and previously rare conditions caused by excessive repetitive movement, like carpal tunnel syndrome, are now common. Good full-time jobs with benefits are on the decline whereas part-time jobs with no benefits are increasing.

Trying desperately to hang on to their standard of living, husbands and wives are working more hours. Author Juliet Schor, in her book *The Overworked American: The Unexpected Decline of Leisure*, tells us that work hours are on the rise:

> In the last twenty years the amount of time Americans have spent at their jobs has risen steadily. Each year the change is small, amounting to about nine hours, or slightly more than one additional day of work. In any given year, such a small increment has probably been imperceptible. But the accumulated increase over two decades is substantial. When surveyed, Americans report that they have only sixteen and a half hours of leisure a week, after the obligations of job and household are taken care of. Working hours are already longer than they were forty years ago.*

---

*J. Schor, *The Overworked American: The Unexpected Decline of Leisure* (Basic Books/Harper Collins, 1991, pp. 1–2).

In late 1990, Mary and I sat down and had a heart-to-heart talk about our future. Our perception of the workplace had changed in the sense that job security didn't exist anymore, and even if it did, we wanted to have more time with each other and with our family. We didn't want our family's financial fate to be in the hands of politicians and chief executive officers (CEOs). Although we both had benevolent employers at the time, there were storm clouds on the horizon. We needed an exit, and as we saw it, the only escape was to save money; enough money to cover most of our basic living expenses for the rest of our lives. But it had to be done quickly because we never knew when the axe would fall. Our mission: to save as much as we could. Fast.

In only 8 years we added over $400,000 to our bottom line on an income (not counting dividends and capital gains) averaging about $65,000 per year. It wasn't easy because we had more expenses than usual during that period. We paid cash for a new car, covered the costs of many medical expenses and orthodontia, helped our daughter pay for her wedding and get a debt-free college education, extensively remodeled our son's room, plus we made some expensive home improvements and repairs like all new kitchen appliances, new roofs, and new central heating and air conditioning. Yet we ended that 8 years with $404,000 more than the $63,000 we started with. We're closing in on half a million just 8 years after we started. In fact, we now have enough to cover the following expenses for the rest of our lives:

- Food
- Clothing
- Shelter
    House
    Heat
    Air conditioning
    Utilities

    Phone
    House maintenance and repairs
    House insurance
    Property taxes
    Appliances
    Household furnishings
    Cable TV
    Internet access
  • Transportation
    Car
    Car insurance
    Car license
    Car maintenance and repairs
  • Dental
  • Miscellaneous expenses
  • Some medical expenses

That's right. We have everything covered now except for part of our medical expenses. In other words, without ever lifting a finger in paid employment, we'll always have hot meals on the table, a car to get where we want to go, and a cozy home to live in. How did we do it? This book will tell you how.

In recent years we have taken our story public in hopes of helping other families achieve financial freedom. After being named among the "Best Personal Finance Managers in America" by *Money Magazine* in 1994, we authored an article that summarized our financial strategies and was published in the April 1997 issue of *Money Magazine*. Some of our strategies were also featured in the February 1998 issue of *McCall's* magazine in an article coauthored by Mary. In 1997, we were invited to share our story at *Money Magazine's* Elgin Project, an event in which *Money* celebrated its 25th anniversary by "adopting" Elgin, Illinois, in an effort to raise the financial I.Q. of an entire community. We have also taken our message to college students in a seminar we've designed specifically for that age group. Unfortunately, our seminars, magazine articles, and newspaper coverage can only scratch the surface of our strategies because of time or space constraints. This book tells it all—how one average family went all the way to financial freedom in only a few short years and how you can do it, too.

Financial freedom is a vague term meaning different things to different people. Some might think they aren't really free unless they're so rich they can buy anything they want while never needing to work again. Is that financial freedom? There are probably some free-spirited vagabonds out there who are free with only a tent and whatever will fit into a backpack. Is that financial freedom? We have given this matter considerable thought in our own situation and arrived at a definition that probably isn't too far off the mark for most families:

> A family has achieved financial freedom when they are able to pay for all of their living expenses, for the rest of their lives, utilizing their assets and 10 to 15 hours of work per week, per spouse, until Social Security, Medicare, and pension eligibility.

Millions of middle-income families can achieve that goal. But wouldn't it be better to pile up enough to be free from the need to work at all? We don't think so. Here's why:

- Work has value beyond a paycheck. We all need to get out of the house and be with other people on a regular basis. Without interpersonal contact, life would be dull, and work provides an excellent opportunity for the regular social interaction we all need.
- The workplace provides access to information. "Who's a good car mechanic?" "Where's the best Italian restaurant in town?"

"Where can I find some professional grade lawn edging?" "I need a pediatrician. Who's good?" We've saved a ton of time and money, and have avoided many headaches by consulting coworkers.

- Work keeps us sharp. It forces us to exercise our brains in complex and rapidly changing situations. It provides stimulating challenges and the opportunity to solve real problems and help others.
- A job provides the opportunity to develop lifelong friendships.
- Work is an excellent way to contribute something to the world. We all want to stand for something and a job is a good place (though certainly not the only place) to do that.
- Work contributes to happiness. In his book *The Pursuit of Happiness: Who Is Happy—and Why?* David Myers states: "Happy, too, are those who gain the sense of control that comes with effective management of one's time. Unoccupied time, especially for out-of-work people who aren't able to plan and fill their time, is unsatisfying. Sleeping late, hanging out, watching TV, leave an empty feeling."*

In my work as a rehabilitation counselor I've learned that most of us really want and need to do some work. People with severe disabilities usually choose to work, even if they have disability income or family support. They may not need employment to pay the bills but still they choose to work. Our 22-year-old son, Tim, is a good example of this. He works part-time as a Wal-Mart greeter. He loves his job and could care less about money. His coworkers are like family to him. What about wealthy people like Bill Gates and Warren Buffett? Surely they don't need to work! But they do. Although many in the workforce may dream of quitting altogether, most who really have the choice to quit, don't. So, we have concluded that, for

---

*D. Myers, *The Pursuit of Happiness: Who Is Happy—And Why* (New York: William Morrow, 1993, p. 116).

us, work is both good and necessary. But there are two problems
with work that just cannot be ignored:

1. Work consumes far, far, too much of our time and life energy.
   As a couple, Mary and I work about 75 hours per week in our
   regular jobs. That doesn't include preparation time, commut-
   ing time (minimal for us, but significant for city dwellers),
   unwinding time, and other work projects, in addition to our
   regular jobs, that we pursue on the side because we love doing
   them. For most of us, work is our life and that's not healthy.

2. When we are totally dependent on a job to provide all of the
   necessities of life for ourselves and our children, we give our
   employers far too much power over us. We've all read about
   factory workers who have wet themselves because they
   weren't granted permission to use the bathroom. We've all seen
   safety violations resulting in injury and death. We've all experienced pressure to be productive or out the door.

The solution? Accumulate enough so you can cover all living
expenses utilizing your assets and 10–15 hours of work per week
per spouse. You'll reap most of the benefits of work while avoiding
most of the problems. You'll be working one or two days a week
and pursuing your passions the rest of the time, while your peers
are slugging it out to hang on to their full-time jobs. Your life will be
better. Less worry, less anxiety, less fear—time to do what you
really want to do. It's possible. You can make it happen.

This book breaks new ground. It is unusual for families with children to accumulate enough wealth to make a difference in a short
time unless they are high earners. Our family has a formula that
works. It could work for your family, too.

Are you a little cynical about the personal finance industry's
hype and exaggerated claims? Does the whole area of personal
finance conjure up negative images of things like boredom, complexity, and hopelessness? If you don't trust professional money
managers but want to know how to manage your money and

achieve more freedom, this book is for you. We have no conflicts of interest. Although we recommend specific investments, we do so only because we feel they're the best. Our strategies are based on real life experiences, involving day-to-day issues faced by most families. Unfortunately, the financial services industry doesn't understand these issues and has left middle-income families behind. They're using strategies designed for the wealthy and applying them to average families even though they usually fail.

This is not a radical or extreme book. It will guide you and your family toward financial freedom using sensible, realistic, logical, and reasonable strategies. Yes, it may seem radical to suggest that families with children earning modest incomes can achieve financial freedom, but we won't propose that you implement extreme changes to get there. In fact, the point of this book is to provide strategies to achieve financial independence *without* earning more money, relocating, or changing jobs. Ours is a moderate, nonthreatening approach. What we have done, you can duplicate, and you won't need to make extensive changes or even suffer to do it.

We won't mislead you by claiming that this process is easy. It's not. Doable, yes. Stimulating, yes. Incredible relief if you make it, yes. Easy, no. For example, some of the concepts you need to learn to invest your money appropriately might be difficult to grasp. But you can do it. All you need to do is read, then read some more, then read some more. When we were just getting started, we took a week off work, got a pile of books, and plowed through them. We can recall the howling wind and subzero temperatures as we sat in our comfy recliners with the pile of books at our sides. It was a week that changed our lives. You can do that. We include a list of excellent, carefully hand-picked resources.

This book is understandable, informal, and conversational: We say what we'd say if you were sitting in our living room. It will challenge you to analyze how you do things and make creative adjustments so you can build assets without suffering. Because you aren't paid a lot, you simply can't afford to make big mistakes with your money, so you need to keep your head in the game and make

8

smart choices. Learning, thoughtful reflection, and creativity lead to smart decisions and financial freedom *without* suffering. Anyone can just stop spending their income and pile up money, but it takes careful planning and creativity to build assets while still enjoying life. We built a large nest egg, we did it fast, and we did it *without* suffering. Your family can do that, too. You, too, can take your average family all the way to financial freedom. This book will show you the way.

PART ONE

BUILDING A
MONEY-SAVING MINDSET

We save a whopping 46 percent of a gross income that isn't very large to begin with and we don't feel any pain. None. How do we do it? Contentment. We're satisfied with what we have, so we can live without almost half of our income and still enjoy life. Tending to happiness is the first big step toward financial freedom. How we think and feel has a great deal to do with our ability to save money, and sometimes we must consciously change our attitudes if we are to have any hope of accumulating enough to make a real difference in our lives. Read on for a discussion of a few key attitudinal issues that have helped us along the road to financial freedom.

LOVE

The Impact of Money on Relationships

There was a movie a few years back whose title I can't remember, but one scene made a big impression. An old, gray-haired man was sitting in silence on a terrace with his wife. He looked into her eyes and asked, "What are your hopes, your fears, your dreams?" She smiled and replied through tears, "I thought you'd never ask."

Bookstores and libraries are stacked to the rafters with books on personal finance and most are about "how." Few even mention "why," but in the end, the "why" is usually about dreams, fears, and hopes.

Like the old couple in the movie, Bill and I sat down one evening when we were in our late thirties and discussed our dreams and fears. Bill's job was threatened by government cutbacks, we had few assets at the time, college costs were looming on the horizon, we needed a new roof and other home repairs, and we had a disabled child who needed considerable care. So we talked late into the night. By daybreak we had decided that we wanted to have more time with each other to do things we never had time to do, to be less dependent on full-time jobs, and have a simple lifestyle that would be played out in a cabin on a lake or somewhere in the woods. In the weeks that followed, we examined every facet of our financial situation—what we spent, where we could cut, and steps we could take to minimize the pain that cutting would cause. We learned as much as we could about personal finance and investing and forged ahead like a house afire. We were determined, enthusiastic, and motivated. In retrospect, there's one thing we did that would be easy to overlook, but it has enabled us to keep moving forward over the long haul: We vowed that financial issues would never drive a wedge between us. Never.

To ensure that wouldn't happen, we made a list of things that could go wrong and we still review that list periodically. We call it our *Killer of Love* list. Here are the killers of love we came up with, each followed by an example of feelings we've vowed we'll never have about each other.

- Killer of love number one is *control.*

  I feel oppressed and controlled. Bill has gone overboard on this spending control and I don't feel like I can spend a dime without getting his approval. I thought this was about financial freedom. It feels more like a financial prison.

- Killer of love number two is the *ball and chain.*

  She doesn't care about me. She just keeps spending and because of her, we'll never get ahead. I don't know if I can stand the thought of working for another 30 years but I'll never be able to get off the treadmill at this rate. She could care less. How could she do this to me?

- Killer of love number three is *the Joneses.*

  Why can't we do things other people do? I'm tired of feeling like the "poor relative." I'm not really a "keep up with the Joneses" type of person, but I do care what people think and I'm sick of feeling like a loser.

- Killer of love number four is *fairness.*

  Yes, I know we're in this together, but why is it that when I want to splurge on something, it's a spending issue and when she wants to spend, it's not?

- Killer of love number five is *it's too hard.*

  I can't stand this. This whole plan to control our spending makes life too grim. This whole thing wasn't my idea anyway. It's just too difficult. I quit!

- Killer of love number six is *it won't work.*

  So we make our lives miserable to save money. Why? We'll never achieve financial freedom anyway, so why are we doing this? I'm unhappy and for what? I'm being pressured to do something I don't want to do; to chase some stupid dream that isn't mine to start with.

- Killer of love number seven is *I'm doing the best I can.*

  I'm the one who handles the spending in the family and I resent it when he implies that I'm spending too much, or that I'm being incompetent when it comes to managing the family's spending. I'm doing the best I can but I'm made to feel like I'm an idiot. To hell with the whole thing!

The road to financial freedom is a long one. It will take several years. Circumstances change. People change. Sometimes even dreams change. But love endures. Our love for each other, our relationship, is our most valued asset. It must be protected and nurtured, because without it there would be no dream, and financial freedom would be an empty shell.

CRISIS

Maintaining Normalcy in a Crisis

We'd had perfect lives until then. Intact, supportive families; good health; strong bodies; happy childhoods in wholesome, carefree small towns; private colleges with postcard-perfect campuses; good friends; and a storybook courtship and wedding followed by a healthy newborn daughter, Colleen.

Then Tim, our second child, was born and something was wrong. He wouldn't eat. He cried a lot. He was kind of floppy, having poor muscle tone. We kept taking him to the pediatrician where he was pronounced healthy. The doctor said things like, "It's just colic." Or, "He's fine." It wasn't colic and he wasn't fine. At 6 months we took him to the hospital. Cardiac arrest. Code blues. Doctors and nurses running. Resuscitations. More codes. More running. More resuscitations. In the midst of it all, we watched, dazed and stunned. We were terrified that Tim would die when a clergyman jogged to the nurse's station and asked, "Where are the parents?"

Tim fought. Hours stretched into days, days into weeks, weeks into months, and months into years. His health problems continued: life-threatening blood pressure spikes that hit him out of the blue, trouble walking, trouble talking, mental retardation, countless crises in the middle of the night, more hospitalizations, and more near brushes with death.

Our perfect lives weren't perfect anymore, but they were better. Perfect really isn't all it's cracked up to be. The adversity we encounter and how we deal with it strengthens and defines us, so now we try to embrace the trials that come our way and turn them into something good. Many families don't survive the pressure of prolonged crises, so we took steps to strengthen our bonds and maintain our sanity while weathering the storm. Looking back on it now, we think these are the strategies that helped most:

- *Make the beds and do the dishes every day, no matter what.* Because your life is chaotic and filled with anxiety, you need to feel that you have some sense of control and order. It is a soothing influence for all. Sometimes these crises last for months or years and you can't give up and let everything fall apart for that long. Besides, if you're busy with menial tasks it helps to keep you from dwelling on the crisis. Anything you do to maintain normalcy will ward off thoughts that "all is lost."

- *Don't forget the children.* They have only one childhood and it goes by quickly. If you have a child in the hospital, one parent should be at the hospital and the other at home tending to the other kids. Attend school events, tuck them in bed at night, read to them, and give them a happy childhood.

- *Don't give in to self-pity or despair.* Accept your fate and move on. Maintain a matter-of-fact attitude. It helps everyone keep their spirits up. It really is possible to maintain serenity when bad things happen.

- *Cook real meals.* It will be tempting to pick up fast food every night, but eating out of a cardboard box is depressing and costs a small fortune if kept up for long. Besides, your family is in crisis. You need each other. Sharing a home-cooked meal is soothing and it's time together to vent, laugh, cry, and plan.

17

- *Don't try to do too much.* Do what's necessary to keep your job, tend to your family, deal with your crisis, enjoy flop time when you can, but no more. Now isn't the time to take on any new projects. You're in water up to your chin already.

Tim is a young man now. His health has improved and he works part-time as a greeter at Wal-Mart. He's just a terrific person who continually makes us proud to be his parents. If you knew him, you'd like him. If we could wave a magic wand and change our son, we wouldn't do it. We like him just the way he is.

We experienced considerable trauma as a young family and it lasted for years, but overall, those experiences have helped us to achieve financial freedom because we don't take anything for granted anymore. Since we never know what tomorrow will bring, we try to be prepared. Furthermore, we've had an incentive to save money so Tim will have something if he outlives us. But most importantly, we're all alive, we're all happy, and we survived as a family. For that we are truly thankful.

COMFORT

How to Be Comfortable in a Modest Home

Shortly after we married we were in the home of a coworker that looked like it came from the pages of a magazine. The place was incredible! We went back to our place feeling like losers but we weren't down for long. We scraped up $50 and decided to redecorate. Fifty dollars was enough to buy a cheap gold area rug and some couch throw covers. When we were done the place looked worse than when we started. We didn't know what we were doing.

A few years later we tried again in a different home. This time we decided to save money by making our own furniture. We bought some furniture-building books and got busy. The pictures in those books made it look so easy, but when we were done, the place looked worse than when we started. This time our furniture was ugly *and* uncomfortable.

A few years later we tried again. We checked out some decorating books from the library. We bought some furniture and when we were done, you guessed it, still ugly. In fact this attempt was the ugliest of all. Well, at least we had comfortable chairs. Ugly, but comfortable.

We forged ahead with a fourth attempt a couple of years later but this time we pulled out all the stops. We actually *read* the decorating books instead of just looking at the pictures. We drew up a detailed floor plan and made a list of things to purchase. At the last minute we decided to ask a decorator to look at our plan and give it her stamp of approval. She looked but she didn't approve. She dumped our plan and started from scratch. When she was done, we had a home we loved and we actually spent less money than we had planned on what would have been our fourth ugly makeover.

We don't want to leave the impression that our home would appear in a magazine or that it impresses our neighbors, because it really is not that type of home at all. It is very modest. But we feel good when we're in our home. Although it isn't flashy, expensive, or extraordinary, it works for us because our decorator knew what we wanted and how to deliver the finished product on our limited budget. During our first meeting with the decorator we provided her with a stack of about 20 pictures we had cut out of magazines. Some were pictures of rooms we liked but one was simply a photograph of a sunset. That told her most of what she needed to know and saved a great deal of time and money because she didn't have to spend time learning about our tastes. Now, when the sun shines into our living room it glows with the colors of the sunset because of the skillful use of color and texture that our decorator employed. The whole effect supports the quiet, peaceful lives we've chosen. Our home is beautiful to us because it meshes very well with our personalities. We're at peace in our home. We feel good there. We like being there.

Interior decorating is an art and most of us aren't artists. If you want to create a sense of well-being, it is important to envelop your family in pleasant surroundings. For most of us, that means hiring a decorator. We were very slow to catch on, so learn from our mistakes.

- Don't try to fix up your place on $50. Save around $5000 so you can buy some quality, durable furnishings and make some small architectural improvements. The key to our living room was a built-in wall unit that cost about $1200.

- While you're saving, familiarize yourself with the decorating process. Watch some of the excellent decorating shows on the Discovery Channel such as the *Christopher Lowell Show, Lynette Jennings Design,* or *Home Matters.* You'll need to understand the basics so you can implement your decorator's plan without hiring someone to do everything.

- Go through old magazines and clip pictures of rooms you like so your decorator will understand your tastes and can plan accordingly.

- Find a decorator who is willing to work with you for an hourly rate. We paid $10 per hour several years ago and used about 10 hours. We saved far more than that by avoiding unnecessary purchases.

- The decorator will tell you what to buy but you should do the shopping yourself. If you find something you like but aren't sure it will fit into your plan, ask the decorator. This is especially crucial for items such as couches, carpet, fabric for curtains, and paint or wallpaper.

- Don't go overboard. Make improvements where you get the most bang for the buck. Move yourself from ugly ("I hate this dump") to comfortable ("wow, that's a lot better!"), but use your resources wisely.

Controlling your spending can be depressing if you don't take steps to bring some beauty and comfort into your life. It is important to improve those areas of your life that undermine your sense of well-being so you won't feel the need to spend money on things that make you feel better. So, bring beauty into your home because you spend so much time there. When you're done, curl up with a good book, play a board game with your children, have a long interesting chat with your husband, prepare a special meal, watch a great movie, or just sit back and experience some quiet solitude in your beautiful, modest home. It is a great (and inexpensive) place to be.

STUDY

How Learning Contributes to Peace, Order, and Financial Freedom

Paul Terhorst changed our family's life forever. Of everyone we have ever encountered in our time on this Earth, Paul is probably in the top ten in terms of impact on our family. And although we owe so much to Paul, we've never met him, never even laid eyes on him. If we saw him on the street we wouldn't know him because we've only had one encounter with Paul, an encounter that took place at our small town's public library. You see, Paul Terhorst wrote a book entitled *Cashing in on the American Dream—How to Retire at 35,* a book I stumbled on one day while browsing through the stacks. At the time I thought the title was a little hokey, and it reminded me of one of those late night infomercials about quick riches. Besides, I had never read a book about finance or business. The topic struck me as boring. So I put it back on the shelf and walked away. But I couldn't find anything else that day so I went back and picked it up. The book was a fast read and from it I carried away only one thing: It doesn't require a huge fortune to achieve financial freedom. I didn't know that. Perhaps I should have known it, but I didn't. One simple concept, one idea set off a series of events that culminated in financial freedom for my family.

Reading is like climbing into someone else's head and snooping around. Frequently it sets off chain reactions that stimulate creativity and improve our lives. We all encounter complex challenges every day—things like building character in our children, diffusing conflicts at home or at work, making ends meet on modest incomes, unraveling health insurance snafus, dealing with unreasonable bosses, or even choosing a long-distance telephone company. It's a complex world and we must be able to think creatively and flexibly or we'll likely fail at these things. Most of us don't have enough personal experiences to draw on, so we read. We get into the heads of others and build on their experiences. Over time we develop a vast network of ideas to draw on.

A few days ago in a discount store, I observed two mothers with five young children. This was a scruffy looking bunch. The mothers were obese, the clothes were dirty, and everyone's hair was stringy and unclean. The children all had blank stares. The mothers took turns screaming, cursing, and swatting at one child or another for some minor infraction. The screams had long ago ceased to have any effect. But the thing that was most striking about these mothers was their remarkable confidence in what they were doing. There was no shame, no embarrassment. It didn't appear to cross their minds that most of the people who were witnessing this spectacle were observing with contempt. But it was the only way they knew, so they were confident that theirs was the only way. They were limited by their own experiences. They didn't read. They didn't study. And their lives were poorer for it.

Until we read Paul Terhorst's book, we thought *our* way was the only way: that we'd work for pay, spend our pay, and keep working until the Social Security Administration said we could quit. We were limited by our own experiences and observations, just like the screaming mothers in the discount store. Writers like Paul Terhorst have changed our lives. But, like the discount store mothers, we still have a long way to go. So we try to read the equivalent of one book per week, covering a wide range of categories such as mysteries, biographies, medical texts, cultural studies, espionage novels, cookbooks, classics, science fiction, inspirational books, and how-to books.

As Mark Twain said, "The man who does not read good books has no advantage over the man who can't read them."

GRATITUDE

Grandma's Red Brick House and Why We Need to Have an "Attitude of Gratitude"

We had just left Grandma's house in Schaller, Iowa, and as we wheeled into the nursing home's parking lot, you could have cut the tension with a knife. She couldn't live alone anymore. She'd handled it fine since Grandpa died 20 years ago, even though her right side had been paralyzed from a stroke for 25 years, but she was too weak to manage it now. She needed help. Now she would live where people go to die. Oh, it was a nice enough nursing home, a sprawling one-story red brick structure with a small, trimmed yard and a well-scrubbed interior. But no matter how you slice it, a nursing home is a depressing place; it's the end of the road. We pulled up to the front door and shut off the ignition. "Well, Grandma, here we are." I don't know what we expected her to say but I'll never forget her response. She said, "All my life I've wanted to live in a big, red brick house."

Most families spend too much. We work too many hours and try to make up for it by splurging. We feel compelled to keep up with our peers. If they have a big new house and cars, then so should we.

And, of course, new and expensive things make us feel good, maybe give us kind of a rush, like any other addictive habit. Gratitude is a key to breaking that cycle.

In his book *How to Want What You Have*, Dr. Timothy Miller states:

> Americans and Western Europeans of the middle class or higher, . . . are among the richest one tenth of one percent of all human beings who have ever lived. Obviously, this wealth can't be measured in dollars or deutsche marks, but it can be measured in terms of freedom from pain and illness, long life, access to recreation, leisure, art, knowledge, survival and health of children, physical comfort, and so on. How often do middle-class people reflect upon this? They are too busy wanting to be one of the richest one hundredth of one percent of all human beings who have ever lived, under the delusion that *then* they will be happy.*

Most baby boomers and thirty-somethings in America today have never experienced poverty firsthand. Poverty to us is a house in need of a coat of paint and a car with a few rust spots. So we all scramble to win a game in which the bar has been set too high. It's tough to conjure up feelings of gratitude while holding yourself to a standard that's impossible to meet. The solution? Change what you think, *not* what you have.

Economist Robert Heilbroner lists what most American families would give up to adopt the lifestyle of a typical family in many countries:

> We begin by invading the house of our imaginary American family to strip it of its furniture. Everything goes: beds, chairs, tables, television, lamps. We will leave the family a few old blankets, a kitchen table, a wooden chair. Along with the bureaus go the clothes. Each member of the family may keep in his "wardrobe" his oldest suit or

---

*T. Miller, *How to Want What You Have: Discovering the Magic and Grandeur of Ordinary Existence* (New York: Avon Books, 1995, pp. 197–198).

dress, a shirt or blouse. We will permit a pair of shoes for the head of the family, but none for the wife or children. We move to the kitchen. The appliances have already been taken out so we turn to the cupboards . . . The box of matches may stay, a small bag of flour, some sugar and salt. A few moldy potatoes, already in the garbage can, must be hastily rescued, for they will provide much of tonight's meal. We will leave a handful of onions, and a dish of dried beans. All the rest we take away: the meat, the fresh vegetables, the canned goods, the crackers, the candy. Now we have stripped the house: The bathroom has been dismantled, the running water shut off, the electric wires taken out. Next we take away the house. The family can move to the toolshed.*

Grandma lived in that nursing home for several years before she died and she was happy there. She enjoyed the company, the recreational activities, and having her meals prepared and served by someone else. It was her home; her big, red brick home. I loved her and I miss her. Whenever I see a nursing home, I think about my Grandma's red brick house. And then I count my blessings. Thank you, Grandma.

---

*R. Heilbroner, *The Great Ascent: The Struggle for Economic Development in Our Time* (New York: Harper & Row, 1963, pp. 33–36).

PART TWO

SPENDING LESS IS EASIER THAN SAVING MORE

Budgets are for sissies. Have you ever heard of the savings concept of "paying yourself first?" That's for sissies, too. Both strategies are based on human weakness instead of empowerment, and neither strategy works. If they did, bankruptcies and personal debt levels wouldn't be so high in this country and savings rates wouldn't be so low. If you're really serious about building a small fortune in a hurry, tap the power within you and control your spending. Examine your big ticket expenses and figure out how to squeeze a fortune out of them using spending strategies that leverage your strengths, not your weaknesses.

SAVING

Why Saving Doesn't Work

This is the wealthiest country in the world, yet we're constantly hearing that families are filing for bankruptcy at record levels and savings rates are at all-time lows. Millions of families are one paycheck away from homelessness. Why is that? Because families don't save enough, right? Well, that seems to be what the pundits say, but we think they have it backward. Spending is the problem, not saving. Telling people to save is like closing the barn door after the horse has already escaped. It's the right thing to do, it's just too late to accomplish anything.

We don't save money. In fact, saving is a bad idea because spending is where the action's at. Saving is what you do with the money left over from spending. We think the whole concept of saving is a crock and we're tired of hearing and reading about the importance of *paying yourself first,* which involves setting aside a fixed amount out of each paycheck. Paying yourself first rests on the assumption that you can *trick* yourself into saving, that if you automatically squirrel away a set amount each month, you won't really see that money, you won't miss it, and you will adjust your spending accordingly. As Colonel Potter on *M.A.S.H.* would say, "Balderdash!" The whole concept of saving a set amount out of your paycheck so you won't notice it buys into the belief that you're weak and unable to control the impulse to spend. So, rather than address that problem head on, experts cooked up the pay yourself first fix. It sounds so easy and clever; it's a catchy, cute-sounding idea, but it doesn't work. If it did, families in this country wouldn't be in such a financial mess. So, we'd suggest that everyone just forget about saving money.

It all comes down to this. If you are going to accumulate enough assets to make a difference in your life, you must spend less than you earn. And if your job doesn't pay all that much to begin with, and you have children, you must spend *far* less than you earn if you're to have any hope of achieving financial freedom. It ain't gonna happen unless you sit down, examine your spending, and figure out how you're going to spend less. Buying your freedom isn't easy and it's not a game for sissies. Getting a handle on your personal finances won't just happen. It is a conscious, thoughtful commitment that takes daily effort and dedication. It isn't painless, but over time you'll adapt and the pain will disappear to be replaced with a tremendous sense of peace and security.

When we were first getting started, we tried the pay yourself first routine. We set aside a certain amount each month and sat back to wait for the money to pile up. It didn't. So we sat down together, examined our spending, identified problem areas, and resolved to cut in some areas and hold the line in others. It wasn't a warm and fuzzy experience, it was just old-fashioned determination and discipline. But it worked. With our first savings plan, we had hoped to have $172,000 in 8 years, but we abandoned that plan and replaced it with a resolve to control our spending and let the chips fall where they may. We're glad we did. In 8 years we ended up with $467,000–almost triple the amount of our original savings goal. Remember, savings plans establish a floor (a minimum amount to save) but they also establish a ceiling (a maximum to save). Why limit the upside?

If you get into an automatic savings plan, you may follow it for awhile, but if you don't learn to control your spending, your bills will accumulate and after a few months you'll decimate your savings to pay those bills and you'll be back where you started. If you really want to be free, do it right. Resolve that you'll never save another dime. Learn how to spend instead. Because you spend every day and save only once; on pay day. It is those numerous spending decisions that will make you or break you.

It is far better to stop the bleeding (control spending) than to start a transfusion (saving). So stop the bleeding.

SPENDING

The Double Whammy
of Spending Control

Back in the mid-1970s, shortly after Saigon fell to the North Vietnamese, I had the privilege of assisting a Vietnamese family who had just landed in the United States. This family was young; the parents were probably in their late twenties and they had two young boys aged about 4 and 5. They spoke no English, of course, and I didn't speak Vietnamese. I helped the family learn some basic English by utilizing flash cards with pictures of common things. I'll never forget holding up a picture of an airplane and hearing the 4-year-old mimic the sound of a machine gun. I could only guess what these people had endured.

Despite their misfortunes and suffering, many Southeast Asians immigrated to this country and did very well. They learned our language, adapted to our culture and climate, followed the rules, and most have become quite productive. I've always had great respect for them, so if I ran across a magazine or newspaper article about Vietnamese-Americans, I tended to read it. One article made a big impression. It described a Vietnamese family who had opened a little neighborhood grocery store in San Francisco. Although their income was small, they lived quite simply and had managed to accumulate about $50,000 in a very short period of time, and they planned to use that money to open another store. The reporter asked them how they tolerated their meager existence. They smiled and politely described what their standard of living had been in Vietnam. They were living high, they said. They were living the good life and couldn't imagine spending more. They were controlling their spending without suffering. It was easy for them.

If you control your spending, two things will happen. First, money will pile up and the earnings on your investments will eventually free you from full-time work. But there's another benefit that's often overlooked. By controlling your spending, you will gradually reduce your needs. If that happens, you won't need to accumulate nearly as much to pay your expenses. In other words, you'll accumulate money faster *and* you'll cut the amount needed to buy your freedom—a double whammy.

Look at it another way. If you want to be able to slam-dunk a basketball, you can strengthen your legs and practice your form. But you can also lower the rim. If your expenses are $50,000 per year, you'll need to save a million bucks or so to support your family with your assets. Most people approach that by trying to scramble up the corporate ladder in hopes of saving money faster. But if that same family learned to be happy with expenses of $25,000 per year, they'd need only $500,000 to support themselves. Plus, since they're now spending only $25,000 a year, they'll have an extra $25,000 each year to invest. So for each dollar they cut from their spending, they've leveraged two dollars. One to invest with the extra savings and another they no longer need because their expenses are lower. Their freedom will be cheaper to purchase, plus they'll get there twice as fast.

We don't usually think about reducing our needs. But if we can do that, if we can really do that, it's as good as doubling the money we have in the bank. When we control our spending, we accumulate assets at the same time that we reduce our needs. It is a powerful combination that leads to freedom.

To that Vietnamese family we read about: if you're out there and you see this, we thank you from the bottom of our hearts for showing us the way to freedom. We'll never forget you.

CATEGORIZE

Categorize Your Spending and Zero In on Problem Areas

I was eleven years old and had just received a present from my dad. It turned out to be the best present anyone ever gave me. One dollar.

I had never had a dollar before, at least not all at once. It was a lot of money for an 11-year-old in those days, so much money that I spent an entire day planning how I'd spend it with the help of my 8-year-old sidekick, brother, and constant companion, Tim. The planning was as exciting as the buying; I can still feel the exhilaration. Thirty-five years later I can still remember some of the things I bought with my dollar. Five red jaw breakers. Five purple jaw breakers. One of those small steel rockets that you put a cap in, throw up in the air, and when it comes down on the sidewalk it goes bang! Then you put two caps in, and then try three, and you keep adding more till no more will fit. Baseball cards. "Archie" comic books. A "Superman" comic book. Some of those straws with that powdery sugary stuff in them. The spending went on for two days. What an incredible time it was.

I'm 47 years old today and I got to thinking about that birthday. I fired up my computer and asked it to tell me how much I have spent in the past few days. $1543.05. And do you know what I spent it on? No, of course you don't. And the sad thing is, neither do I. I can remember how I spent one dollar 36 years ago, but I don't have a clue how I spent $1543.05 last week. To 47-year-olds, spending money is just another chore to check off the list.

There's a real danger in that, isn't there? We've become completely detached from the spending decisions we make. It's all been placed on a kind of autopilot. If we think we need it, we buy it. If we want it, we buy it. A bill is due, we pay it. But it's all kind of automatic. Boring. Sometimes we even sign on to automatic bill paying services. The money is zapped out of our account; it just disappears all by itself. So why are we surprised that there never seems to be any money left to save when we don't pay attention to what we spend?

If you're really serious about changing your life and becoming more financially independent, you need to start paying attention, and you can do that by keeping track of what you spend. Here's how:

First, sit down with a pen and paper and make a list of where your money goes, a list of spending categories. To help you get started, here are ours:

Appliances

Cable TV

Cars (to purchase and to maintain)

Car insurance

Car license

Charity

Christmas presents

Internet

Clothing

Home decorating

Dental

Utilities

Food

Heat

Miscellaneous

Eye glasses

Birthday presents

House insurance

House maintenance

Life insurance

Phone

Property tax

School lunches

Vacations

Medical

Union dues

Federal tax

State tax

FICA

Next, print a small list of your categories and tape it to your check register. Every time you make a purchase, note the category in your check register. Let's say you spend $40 in a department store. Several packages of toilet paper cost $5, oil for the car costs $10, and for a prescription you pay $25. Your check register entry would look like the accompanying sample entry.

At the end of the month, transfer all the information from your check register to your favorite personal finance computer program

Sample Check Register Entry

Check No.	Date	Payee	Payment	Deposit	Balance
7512	10/24/98	Wal-Mart	$40.00		$348.78
		5-misc, 10-car, 25-medical			

(Quicken, Microsoft Money, etc.). Print itemized category reports each month and examine them closely. Ask questions such as:

- Where is our money going?
- Do we really need to spend so much on this?
- Oh, no, we've spent twice as much on heat this December as last December. Should we fix that window?
- Our food costs have increased 50 percent. Why?

Plan carefully and spend like an 11-year-old. Buy the things you'll remember in 36 years. If you can't remember what you bought last week, there's a good chance some of your money is being wasted. Find that money. Keep it. Invest it. Eventually it will buy your freedom.

SURPRISE

Avoiding the Trap of Failing to Plan for All Expenses

When we were in our twenties, we worried a lot about money. Of course, in those days, we really didn't have much to spare, but we had enough to cover our expenses. Having enough didn't matter though. We worried anyway. Eventually we came up with a simple system that eased our anxiety, and although we didn't know it at the time, it laid the groundwork for a future of financial freedom. In retrospect, our little system was probably the most important fiscal strategy we ever implemented. If we hadn't done it, we probably wouldn't be writing this book today.

If your salary just doesn't seem to stretch far enough, you might be making the same mistake we made: failing to plan for *all* expenses. Most of us tend to plan for the expenses that we must deal with on a regular basis, such as:

Cable TV

Car payments

Clothing

Food

Heat

Internet

Miscellaneous/personal

Phone

Rent/mortgage

Utilities

However, we often forget to address some of the hidden costs of living, such as:

Appliances

Birthdays

Car insurance

Car license

Car maintenance and repairs

Charity

Christmas

Decorating

Dental

Federal taxes

FICA

Eye glasses

House insurance

House maintenance

Life insurance

Medical

Property taxes

School lunches

State taxes

Vacations

So we go merrily along with money in our pockets and *Whap!* We're slammed in the side of the head with an expense we had forgotten about—one of the kids needs new glasses, the property tax bill is due, and the refrigerator is dead. Now we're right back in the hole again. It seems that every time we manage to have a little left over at the end of the month, we get hit again, and unless we do something about it, we'll never get ahead.

How can that cycle be broken? We suggest that you make a list of every foreseeable expense. Every single one. When you're done, assign a monthly cost to each one, and when you get your paycheck, either pay the expense if it's due, or set aside a small amount that will accumulate over time. When it's time to pay the piper, you'll have the cash to do it.

How can you assign a monthly expense to something like appliances? This isn't an exact science by any means, but we expect to spend about $30 a month on appliances like refrigerators, microwaves, TVs, VCRs, stereos, stoves, garbage disposals, dishwashers, dehumidifiers, range hoods, and so on. We arrived at that figure by estimating that we'd probably need to replace all of our appliances in about a decade at an average cost of about $360 each if we bought everything new at once. If we own 10 major appliances, that's an average of one appliance per year. Divide $360 per year by 12 months and you have $30. So with each paycheck (we just happen to get paid roughly twice a month), we set aside $15 to cover appliance costs that we *know* we'll be clobbered with in the future. Of course, we may not buy a single appliance for the next several years because most of ours are relatively new, but in 8 years they could start dropping like flies. When they do, we'll be ready. No more anxiety.

We used to go to the bank and borrow money for a car, but now we pay cash. We set aside $143 a month. We purchase a new car about every 7 years. If a new car costs $12,000 and we keep it for 7 years, we'll average $1714 a year or $143 a month. Because we pay cash, there are no monthly car payments or interest expenses. How about car repairs? Ah, this is where it really pays to categorize and track spending. We simply fired up the computer and calculated that we had actually spent $2565 over a 4-year period on car maintenance and repairs. Divide that by 48 months for a total of $53 a month. That's what we set aside for car maintenance and repairs.

We spend $75 a week on food. That's $300 a month, right? Wrong. There are 52 weeks in a year and $75 times 52 is $3900. Divide $3900 by 12 months for a monthly food budget of $325. We tend to think there are 4 weeks in a month but that lops 4 weeks off the year. I'd get mighty hungry in 4 weeks, wouldn't you? Keep that in mind when you're estimating what to save for weekly expenses.

We're sold on the idea of foreseeing and saving for *all* expenses for three reasons. First, it prevents underestimating expenses and eliminates the need for credit cards. We hate credit cards. Second, it decreases anxiety. Life is just too short to worry about money. And finally, if you start setting money aside for anticipated future expenses, you'll probably overestimate your needs. In a short time you'll have several thousand dollars in the bank. You'll be on the way to financial freedom. That's how we got started. Nowadays, the only surprises at our house are delivered by a fat man in a red suit. Ho! Ho! Ho!

BORROWING

Despising Debt

I was reading a newspaper today and the article quoted a famous billionaire who was promoting an aggressive expansion of international free trade. That's not surprising: Free trade is widely viewed as a means of raising the world's standard of living, especially the worlds of billionaires. What *did* surprise me was what the billionaire suggested we do about Americans who lose their jobs to falling trade barriers. He pushed for taking very good care of those people.

Shortly after seeing that article I flipped on the tube and listened to a prominent conservative congressman tick off a short list of pressing government business, which included weighty issues like saving social security, rescuing Medicare, and bankruptcy reform. Bankruptcy reform? Is that what the good old boys in the coffee shops are wrestling with these days? "I don't know about you, Jim Bob, but if they don't deal with bankruptcy reform, they'll lose my vote." Out of curiosity I fired up the computer, logged on to the Internet, punched in "bankruptcy," and sure enough, corporate lobbyists are pushing changes that would make it easier for businesses to collect what they are owed in the wake of skyrocketing bankruptcies.

I turned off the computer, picked up the paper again, and read that business lobbyists "ran the table"* during the most recent legislative session, winning approval for more employee drug testing as well as unemployment and workers' compensation changes tilted in favor of employers.

So within about 20 minutes, without even trying, I was bombarded with information that screams, *now is a dangerous time for families to accumulate debt!* Free trade will expand and wipe out more jobs, our society should but doesn't take good care of people who lose those jobs, employer-paid lobbyists are in charge of writing work-related legislation, and bankruptcy changes are imminent while the numbers of families seeking bankruptcy protection are exploding. All of this is happening against a backdrop of a social security system that is teetering on the brink, in a country where medical care is reserved for those who can afford to buy it. These trends threaten debt-burdened families.

We despise debt. Debt is the opposite of financial freedom. It's financial slavery. To us it is an anathema; it's like toxic waste that exists only to be cleaned up. Debt is spending your future; it's digging a hole and climbing in.

In a seminar prepared for college students, we describe debt in terms of french fries. "Most of you are 19 or 20," we say to them. "Let's say you've got a hankering for a serving of fries and it costs a buck at the local burger joint. Is it worth a dollar? Yes, it probably is. But what if you borrow the dollar at 9 percent and carry that debt until you're our age? By then you'd owe more than $10. Are the fries worth $10? No, of course not. Well, 9 percent is the going rate now for those nifty home equity loans everybody seems to be touting. What if you use your credit card to pay for the fries and carry the debt at 18 percent? By the time you're our age," we tell them, "you'll owe $87. But, you might be thinking that you'd never

---

*A billiards term meaning that the player put all the balls in the pockets without losing a turn. In this case it means that the lobbyists won all they were trying for.

borrow money for french fries. No? Well, think about it. If you always carry a balance on your card, like many families do, you could reduce that debt by a dollar if you pass on those fries, couldn't you? So when you buy them, you're making a decision to keep a dollar of debt at 18 percent when you could pay it off instead. How is that any different than buying french fries on credit? It isn't. A serving of fries for $87. Wow. That's a lot of money for one serving of french fries."

Although there's no such thing as good debt, some debts are better than others. College loans make sense if there's no other way to get a degree. The only thing worse than being buried under a mountain of college debt is to try to make your way through life as an unskilled worker. Who can compete with overseas workers earning 50 cents an hour? I'd choose the college loans.

For a very select few, borrowing to set up a small business might be worthwhile, but most business startups fail.

Of course, most of us will need to borrow for a home, and although a mortgage is usually a necessity, the value of the tax deduction on mortgage interest is overplayed. Sure, it's nice to get the tax break, but you're still forking over your hard-earned cash for the privilege of using someone else's money. It's wise to get out from under that burden as fast as you can. We've heard people say that they plan to get a home equity loan (a loan using equity in your home as collateral) because they need a tax deduction. Those loans might reduce your tax bill but the interest costs will far exceed any tax savings. And what about your 401(k) at work? Should you contribute to the retirement plan or accelerate the house payments? Well, that's what we call a hair-splitting question that requires both a computer and a crystal ball, so we almost always lean toward paying off the house, unless the 401(k) involves an employer match. Always take full advantage of the match.

A car loan is the next rung down on the debt desirability list. Like a mortgage, most of us can't afford to pay cash for a car, but that's where the similarity ends. Interest on a car loan is not tax deductible and cars aren't investments that hold their value over time, like houses usually do. A car is a piece of junk waiting to happen, so borrowing to own one is a bad financial move that most of us are forced to take. Plan to pay it off as fast as you can (never more than 4 years) and plan to pay cash for cars by the time you're 45.

Credit card debt is as bad as it gets if you don't count loan sharks. We've carried an occasional credit card for emergencies but we've never actually used one. With interest rates in the high teens, they make no financial sense. If you're paying credit card interest you're either throwing money away or you're in financial trouble. Your best move? Cut them up.

If debt is a problem for you, it means you're spending more than you earn. Maybe you've lost your job, encountered uninsured medical problems, or had some financial catastrophe. That certainly is not your fault and you have our sympathy. Maybe you're young and just getting started on your own. That can be difficult and it will take awhile to get on your feet, so don't feel bad if you're forced to borrow for awhile. Or maybe you just haven't been willing to live within your means. You want the best and aren't willing to wait, to substitute good for best, or to substitute fair for good.

- No way! I want a house with a family room and at least two bathrooms.

- That car isn't very comfortable. Let's buy that deluxe model.

- A public college for my little darling? You've got to be kidding!

- I really, really need that video accelerator and another 64 meg of RAM.

- I don't care if we are in debt. I just worked my tail off to get a college degree and I'm not having second-hand furniture in my living room.

47

- We just can't have a wedding for less than $10,000. It's unheard of!
- Let's go out to eat. Taco Bob's?? You're kidding, right?

If you're carrying a big debt load because you just can't live without the best, there's only one escape. Change your mindset. Debt problems usually don't have anything to do with financial issues. They are purely psychological issues and like any addiction, materialism is tough to break, especially when advertisers spend billions to entice. But debt is financial slavery. It is the opposite of financial freedom and cannot coexist with it. If you want to eliminate it once and for all, consider our Seven Steps to Eliminate Debt:

1. *Acknowledge that you have a problem.* "I guess I am spending more than I earn. I created the problem and I can fix it."
2. *Decide.* "I don't want to live from paycheck to paycheck under a pile of debt. I'm sick of the anxiety. I want financial freedom."
3. *Tune out all the background noise.* "Television ads tell me that I only live once so I should go for the gusto, but I'd rather have freedom, so I won't listen."
4. *Make it mutual.* "I can't do it alone. We need to be together on this and we must do it fairly. For every dollar he cuts, I'll cut one, too."
5. *Fire up!* "It is possible to be debt-free in 5 years. We've crunched the numbers, hashed out the details, and we know we can do it. After that, we'll start piling up the savings and in another 5 years we'll be able to reduce our work load. Hooray!"
6. *Embrace discomfort.* "Nothing worthwhile comes easily, we know that. But we're tough. We can cut it. Besides, we've made plans to enjoy life, too, so it won't be unbearable. In a few months, we won't even miss the things we are cutting."

7. *Learn how to be grateful.* "Aren't we lucky to be sitting in our warm house when it's twenty below outside? Come here and look at this beautiful sunset. Isn't life great? Aren't we lucky? Look at all we have."

Debt robs you of choices, chains you to employment whether you want it or not, contributes to an escalating dependency on nice things, and slowly bleeds away your capacity to enjoy. It's poison. Obliterate it from your life.

CREEP

The Perils of Increasing Your Standard of Living Too Quickly

Most of us increase our standard of living as fast as our pay-checks will let us and, to be fair, it isn't entirely our fault. It all starts when we're young. There's that first job at the bottom of the pay scale, an overpriced apartment that needs furnishing, a mountain of college debt, that first car with eye-popping insurance rates, and before too long, a child on the way. In other words, a financial quagmire; more expenses than income. So we spend every dime we have, and then some, just to survive. A few years later, we scrape together enough for a down payment on a house while still whittling away at our college loans. By this time we might have another child or two. We've been struggling to improve our lot in life; moving from a fringe area to a safe neighborhood, finally getting a reliable car, or maybe even buying a couch that hasn't been owned by 10 people before us. Now we're used to improving our standard of living as fast as possible and that's a good thing. We can't live in poverty forever.

There comes a point in life, probably in our early thirties, when further embellishments have more to do with status or comfort than with necessity. But we usually don't recognize that moment, that crossover, so we keep right on spending. We've been under the gun to build a better life since leaving our parents. It's all we know, so the spending continues. There's no finish line, so we don't know when to slow down. But some families are able to perceive this crossroads. If these families have the desire to achieve financial freedom and possess the discipline to rein in their spending, they will succeed.

It's tough to slam on the brakes after growing accustomed to moving up to bigger, better, newer, nicer, cooler stuff. Here are three strategies we have used to make it easier:

1. We have a dream to be free from dependence on full-time employment and to have a cabin on a lake. We visualize life in our cabin; what we'll be doing, what the cabin will look like, the things we'll do. It is a life we choose, a life we designed, one that fits perfectly. That dream, that life, is worth more to us than having a bigger house or a fancier car today.

2. It's easy to feel deprived when we're surrounded by an endless array of nice things we want. Many families succumb to those feelings as evidenced by skyrocketing debt and bankruptcy and dismal savings rates. But if we feel deprived, the solution is not to feed our deprivation, because that simply accelerates the process and becomes a vicious circle. The solution is to heap more deprivation upon ourselves so that we will no longer feel impoverished when we return to baseline. Feel like your house is a dump? If you have a daughter in college, go spend a few days in her apartment. Sleep on the floor. She'll have no air conditioner, of course, so go in the summer when it's 95 degrees and humid. Watch the old TV that gets one channel. Then go home, turn on your central air, choose from 40 channels on any of your three TVs. You won't feel impoverished anymore. Spending a few days with your daughter is a lot cheaper than building a new house.

3. When you visit friends who live like kings, don't feel inferior. Realize that while you control your destiny, they probably don't. Your family is building financial security, theirs probably isn't. You may stop working early, they probably won't.

These things we need; everything else is optional:

- Food
- Clothing
- Shelter
- Medical care
- Safety (from crime, hazards, etc.)
- Education
- One reliable car
- A few personal items

If we have the basic necessities of life, most of the rest is about status and comfort. We'd rather have freedom. It's better.

PART THREE

NECESSITIES AND
A FEW EXTRAS

Follow the money. For many, that line conjures up images of two young *Washington Post* investigative reporters digging into the Watergate scandal. If they could trace the path of the money, it would lead them to the White House. So they followed the money. We followed the money, too, but it didn't lead to the White House. By focusing on the big ticket necessities of life and a few extras, we ended up with $467,000 in our pockets in only 8 years. Tell you what, Bob and Carl, you can have the White House. We'll take the money. Read on to learn how you can follow the money to financial freedom.

HOME

Choosing the Right House Will Make You or Break You

This is our house. It isn't an impressive house, is it? You've seen a million just like it, and it probably isn't on anyone's dream house list. It's just, well, kind of average. So why do we like this house so much?

For starters, we estimate that we have over $100,000 in our pockets now because of this house. We paid $40,000 for it in 1982. We thought about buying an $80,000 house but decided to be conservative and by spending less we were able to pay off the house in only 10 years. We estimate that we've saved $55,000 in interest alone by going with the smaller house.

When we paid off our mortgage we didn't stop making the monthly payments. That's right, we continued to make the mortgage payments, but we paid ourselves instead of the bank. So all that interest that we'd have sent to the bank for another decade or so, if we had chosen the expensive house, has gone directly to our bottom line instead. Furthermore, we've paid far less for property taxes, insurance, maintenance, furnishings, heating, and electrical because our home is smaller. More than $100,000 so far and more on the way! Oh yeah, we love this house.

Our house is in a small Iowa town of about 6000 and life here hasn't changed much since the days of Ozzie and Harriet. The schools here are very good. We don't have major crime or drug problems. We take walks late at night without fear. Choosing a safe neighborhood to live in is not a concern because all neighborhoods are safe in our town. It's just a great place to live. Traffic is a nonissue. We reside only 5 minutes from work, maybe 6 minutes tops, so we come home for lunch every day.

Choosing a home will likely be the single most important financial decision you will ever make, so it is important to do it right. If you choose a large home adjacent to a golf course, you probably won't achieve financial freedom until the Social Security Administration decides to let you quit your job. Most of your extra money will be poured into mortgage interest. The interest on a $200,000 home at 8 percent for 30 years is about $328,000. That is money paid to the bank when much of it could have been paid to you instead. Let's say you buy a $60,000 house instead, and you pay it off in 10 years, running up about $28,000 in interest. You'd save $300,000 on interest alone! And don't forget, even more costly than the loss of the $300,000, is the loss of all the money that the $300,000 could have earned for you over the course of your lifetime. But you don't want to live in a hovel on a block infested by drug dealers and crack houses just to save money. So what should you do? Here are some strategies to consider.

Get a job with a large corporation, or a state or federal agency that has branch offices in rural areas. You'll probably be required to start working in a metro area because that's where most of the openings will be, but after a couple years, transfer to a small town. Salaries are usually set at company headquarters in a city where expenses are high, but you'll be earning the same in Pisgah as your colleagues are making in Chicago. You'll have the salary of a metro dweller, the expenses of a villager, better schools, and less crime.

Buy a home that you can pay off by age 45. That will keep you in a smaller house with lower taxes, insurance, maintenance, heat, utilities, and furnishings. Before you know it, you'll be sending those monthly payments to yourself instead of the bank. There's nothing quite so gratifying as the feeling of owning your home, free and clear, while piling up money at the same time. If you've already purchased a $200,000 house, all is not lost. If you're in a hot real estate market, consider selling it for a profit and buying a more affordable home. If you can't do that, accelerate the payments. It's the interest that kills you, so you need to get the debt paid off as soon as you possibly can.

Try to buy in a neighborhood where other homes are predominantly more expensive than yours. You don't want to own the best house on the block because the other houses will diminish the value of yours. Avoid buying near rentals. Check out the neighbors, the schools, tax rates, crime rates, and utility costs.

Buy a modest home in Pisgah, decorate it, and stay put. Don't dash off to a bigger, better house as soon as you accumulate some extra money or unused credit. Who are you trying to impress?

Above all, buy your home with financial freedom in mind. That dream house could plunge you into years of financial insecurity and anxiety while keeping you in the harness until you're in your seventies. If you buy that big, fancy house you will probably forfeit some of the best years of your life to pay for it. It's just not worth it. You can have a very fulfilling, happy, and comfortable life in a modest home.

WHEELS

Car-Buying Secrets

"Good afternoon, sir. Welcome to Billy Bob Honda. My name's Biff Slicker. How can I help you today?"

"Well, Biff, I want to buy a car. I'm not sure what I need, but I need the car today since my old car broke down and it's not worth fixing. I've got $8000 for a down payment and my monthly payments can't be more than $500. I'd like to get it financed here so I can have my car today."

"We'll do the best we can to put you in a car today. By the way, what's your name?"

"Jay."

"Well, Jay, today is your lucky day. Hey, that rhymes, doesn't it? Ha, ha. I've got the perfect car for you."

You've just witnessed a car salesman's dream. Jay is about to pay far more for a car than necessary; in fact, some salesmen even have an expression for what is about to happen to Jay. They refer to it as "tearing his head off." Jay did everything wrong before the salesman even knew his name. Let's break it down and examine Jay's mistakes.

- *"I'm not sure what I need . . ."* This tells the salesman that you don't know what you want. He'll choose a car for you but he isn't looking out for your interests. It's his job to make a profit for himself and his dealer. If you give him complete discretion, if you don't box him in, he'll propose options that put you in the least amount of car for the most amount of money.

- *"I need the car today . . ."* You're desperate. You'll pay more for less.

- *". . . my old car broke down and it's not worth fixing."* You're really desperate! Furthermore, the salesman knows you hate the old car that put you in this position, so you'll probably accept less when you trade.

- *"I've got $8000 for a down payment . . ."* You're pretty savvy with your finances and you know it's smart to avoid debt whenever possible, so you've socked away a pretty big down payment. And you are smart to do that. But there's a downside you need to be aware of. Let's say you choose a car worth $15,000. You haven't done any research so you end up agreeing to pay $20,000 for the car. If your down payment is $3000, you'll need to finance $17,000 but the bank won't do it. There's no way they'll loan $17,000 for a car worth only $15,000. But if you have an $8000 down payment, the bank will put up the remaining $12,000. The deal will sail through. So although it's a good idea to put up as much cash as possible, make sure you know what the car is worth before you buy.

- *". . . my monthly payments can't be more than $500."* There's a rule of thumb in the car business: $25 per month for every $1000 financed. So when you tell the salesman you want your payment to be $500 per month, he does the mental math in a nanosecond; you can afford to finance $20,000. With an $8000 down payment, he'll get $28,000 out of you. Now all he needs to do is find the least amount of car you'll accept for $28,000. To make it more palatable for you he'll "load the payment," which means that he'll add things you don't need like extended warranty, rustproofing, and extra interest. Before you know it, you've spent $28,000 on an $18,000 car. Granted, he won't be able to sell you a car worth less than the bank will finance, but your $8000 down payment provides plenty of room to "tear your head off."

- *"I'd like to get it financed here . . ."* It's usually not a good idea to finance your car through the dealership. Use your credit union or bank. They have advertised interest rates and you can shop around for the best deal. If you finance through a dealer, they might jack up the rate to fit your monthly payment. Dealers buy their financing from banks and if you're gullible enough to pay more than the going rate, the dealer sometimes splits the excess with the bank. So, if you finance through a bank you'll get the bank's advertised rate. Finance through a dealer and the very same bank will likely split the proceeds of your ignorance with the dealer. That's right. Bankers will let the car store increase the rate behind the scenes and share the excess profit with the dealer. If a dealer is offering low interest rates as an incentive, that might be a reason to finance there. But if there's a choice between a factory rebate and a low rate, it's usually better to take the rebate if the math is close. Then if you decide to trade in a year or two, you won't lose what you'd planned to save on interest. But if you do choose the low interest, there's one other tidbit you might not be aware of. If you finance through a dealer and you have a stellar credit rating, the dealer might "piggyback" your good credit with that of another customer who has marginal credit in order to close the deal with the other customer. The dealer will send both loan requests to the bank. If the banker calls the dealer and says he'll do your loan, but not the other guy's, the dealer might tell the banker he doesn't get your loan unless he accepts both. If the banker still refuses, the dealer will call another bank, and that could be a problem for you if the next bank agrees but charges a higher rate than the first. Your good credit might help the dealer make a bundle and cost you in the process. Something to keep in mind and perhaps another reason not to finance through a dealer.

So, what's a good way to buy a vehicle? Well, the first step is to decide whether to get new or used. We usually choose to go with new. I know, I know; experts often say that you'll spend less in the long run if you buy used and I'm sure that's probably true, especially if you trade every two or three years, but they are usually talking about mid- to high-priced cars and not the $10,000 models we buy. Besides, a car is just a way to get from here to there and our small gas sippers will carry us as far as the $25,000 deluxe models. After 10 years or so, an economy car and a plush sedan are worth about the same, somewhere between a thousand bucks and nothing. So we buy inexpensive cars with good track records for reliability and drive them for about 14 years. We have two cars and about every seven years we buy a new car, and sell the oldest one ourselves. Then we have a new car that we use for highway trips, and a 7-year-old car with about 84,000 miles on the odometer. We relegate that car to town driving only, so it accumulates only a couple thousand miles per year. After about 7 years, we sell it ourselves and buy another new one. Another reason we prefer new cars is because we don't want to put up with the breakdowns that are more likely to occur with used cars. Life is too short. Furthermore, we're almost fanatical about car maintenance and almost never have breakdowns. We attribute that, at least in part, to good maintenance. With a used car, there's no way of knowing if it has been neglected or abused.

Next, choose the specific make and model. It's a good idea to select a model that has been around long enough to have a track record. We'll consider a car that has been on the market for at least 5 years but only if it's been at least 2 years since the model has been redesigned. We check the car's reliability in *Consumer Reports* magazine, but verify their findings with other sources at the local library and on the Internet. There's helpful information on the Internet at www.consumerworld.org. We choose two or three reliable models to test drive and then check on insurance rates to narrow the choice to one.

Now determine what you are willing to pay for the car. Plan to pay about 2–3 percent (for us that's about $200–300) over the invoice. (The invoice price is what the dealer paid for the car.) Two to three percent over the dealer's cost doesn't sound like much, but dealers usually get a 2–3 percent "holdback" from the manufacturer. You'll also pay a destination charge, taxes, and license. Dealer invoice amounts are widely publicized. You'll find them in the car issues of financial magazines like *Money* and *Kiplinger*, or you can get them on the Internet at www.edmunds.com. If the dealer invoice is $10,063, you'd tack on 2 percent ($201) and the destination charge ($415) and offer to pay $10,700. If you do the math, you'll come up with $10,679, but it's a good idea to round up to the nearest hundred. Always round up. If you don't, the salesman will think you're a pain and you'll be less likely to close the deal.

Once you've determined what you're willing to pay, you're ready to visit the dealer, but before you do, it might be helpful to examine your attitude about car salesmen. Remember, they are real people with wives or husbands, parents, children, brothers, sisters, and friends. Most make good money, but they work brutal hours, often in hostile, adversarial environments. They're just trying to support themselves and their families. They're working in tough jobs that most of us couldn't tolerate. So don't go in there with an attitude. Treat them with courtesy and respect. Show some interest in them as people. If you do, you'll stand out and they'll appreciate it. You'll feel better, too, and the whole experience will be more pleasant.

Shop for your car between 10:00 A.M. and 3:00 P.M. Tuesday through Friday. Never go in on Saturday. That's when most customers buy cars and sales staff are swamped. Don't shop for a car on Monday either because they are busy doing paperwork for deals that closed on Saturday, and serving customers who shopped Saturday, went home to think about it over the weekend, and then returned to buy on Monday. Business is usually slow Tuesday through Friday during the middle of the day when most people are at work. OK, you're ready. It's time to hit the showroom floor.

"Good afternoon, sir. Welcome to Billy Bob Honda. My name's Biff Slicker. How can I help you today?"

"Biff, my name is Jay. Let's sit a minute."

"Sure. Come on in here."

"Biff, I'll be up front with you. I'm gonna be a very easy customer to deal with. I know your time is valuable so I won't waste it. I've decided to buy a new (insert name of your car here) and I'll pay $10,700 plus tax and license. I realize you won't make enough on the deal to get too excited about it, but I promise you two things. First, I know the customer satisfaction survey is important to you and I promise that I'll give you the highest ratings possible if I buy this car. Second, I won't be a pain and waste your time. I'll take any color you have on the lot and I don't want any options. I'm in no hurry to buy, so if you've got some quota to make in the next week or two and I can put you over the top, I'll hold off until you need the sale. Now, if you can do this deal today, that would be great. Or, if you're willing to do it but today isn't the best for you, just tell me and I'll come back later. All I'll need is an hour notice and I'll be here with a check. I want to do whatever works for you."

"Jay, I don't think I can do it for $10,700 but I might be able to convince my sales manager to go for $11,100."

"I know you won't make a lot on this deal, Biff, but you're guaranteed some profit plus the holdback, and I really am sincere about the consumer satisfaction survey. When I'm done with the survey they'll be looking at you for canonization. Plus, I'll recommend you to my friends. Here, take my card and call me if you change your mind. I know you won't make a lot on this deal, Biff, but I promise I'll make it a fast and easy one. I've already taken up enough of your time (as I'm getting out of my chair). Thanks for hearing me out and please do call if you're willing to do this deal. In fact, I'll give you some time to think it over so you can time this sale however it works best for you. I won't make the same offer to other dealers for a week so you have a chance to work it out. Thanks, Biff."

At this point you leave. Now wasn't that easy? The whole exchange took less than five minutes. There was absolutely no negotiation. You set a positive tone. The exchange was pleasant with none of the typical anxiety or adversarial banter. The salesman knows you'll make the same offer to other dealers and he'll probably call and agree to accept your offer. Eventually, you'll get your car at a good price without going through the usual tortuous process that everybody hates. It's a great way to buy a new car.

It's preferable to send one person to close the deal, so for married couples, who should go? Most of us have probably heard at one time or another that women aren't taken seriously by car salespersons. Our sources tell us that is no longer true. In fact, sales staff are trained to be sensitive to these outdated public perceptions. Women might actually have a slight advantage on that basis alone. So send whoever is most comfortable in this type of situation.

If you're intent on getting a used car, you'll want to proceed in a similar fashion. It's tougher to do, though, because there's no consumer satisfaction survey on used cars and you won't know what the car is worth. To determine the car's worth, check the National Automobile Dealers Association's (NADA) *Appraisal Guide*, but be sure to use the version the car dealers and banks use, not the Consumer Edition. Realize that the NADA prices are frequently way off the mark in either direction, so if you're buying or selling a used car, do what some of the pros do to determine the car's value. Get out the classifieds, find ads for your model, and call the seller who's asking the highest price. Ask if the car has sold. It probably hasn't. Call the owner with the next lower asking price and ask the same question. Keep calling until you've found one that has sold. Whether you are buying or selling, the vehicle's value is probably somewhere between the price of the car that has sold and the one with the next highest price that hasn't. This is a bit of a hassle, but NADA prices can be hundreds of dollars off. A half-hour on the phone could save you a bundle.

How about one-price stores? Companies like Saturn slap nonnegotiable prices on their cars. Salespersons there aren't paid commissions. We don't buy our cars that way and don't recommend it unless you're determined to get a Saturn or you're a terrible negotiator. In those places, everybody ends up with a C minus deal. If you're an A plus negotiator, why settle for a C minus? If you want to pay a thousand dollars over invoice on a $10,000 car, power to you. We don't buy cars that way. It's too expensive.

Some families hate negotiating so much that they hire a car broker to do the buying for them. Just remember that the broker's services aren't free. Most of them are paid commissions, too. But cost isn't the only disadvantage. If you've purchased a car directly from a dealer, and you've given the salesman top ratings on his consumer satisfaction survey, he'll remember you and be your advocate if you get jacked around by the service department. Who will help you if you buy through a broker?

It is possible now to buy a new car over the Internet for a very reasonable price. Check out www.carsdirect.com. They will quote a price instantly and deliver the car to your door in some locations. This is probably the wave of the future, but don't expect red carpet treatment at your local dealer if you buy over the Internet and get stuck with a lemon. If you aren't comfortable buying a car this way, consider checking the price of the car you want at carsdirect.com or a similar site, and then use that price to negotiate with your dealer.

Car dealers make money two ways, on the front end (what you pay for the car over the dealer's cost) and on the back end (things like credit life/accident/health, extended warranties, interest mark-ups, and rustproofing). Most customers expend all their emotional energy on the front end, so there's a letdown after the deal is closed. Your guard is down. But it's not uncommon for car stores to net $200 on the front and $1500 on the back, so don't relax your vigilance after you've settled on a price for the car. Just say, "No, thank you." If you're really sold on rustproofing, negotiate up from the dealer's cost of about $100. Don't pay more than $200.

We've saved a lot of money on cars over the years and you can, too. All it takes is a little research, a little confidence, and a big desire for financial freedom. You can do it!

Supermarket

How a College Class Assignment Changed Our Approach to Grocery Shopping

Several years ago Bill's sister, Maureen, told me about a college project she had just finished for a Home Economics/Nutrition class. They were studying the lives of welfare families and one of the students insisted that there was no way that a family of four (three children and a mother) could survive on a meager welfare check. So the class set out to break down all of the basic survival expenses and when they were done they had $25 per week left over for food. Then the professor gave the class this assignment: Go forth into the grocery stores of Ames, Iowa, and prepare a nutritionally sound menu for four people on only $25 per week. No garden, no bulk buying, no canning, no large freezer. Just go to the store with an imaginary $25 and do the best you can.

Impossible? Surprisingly, no. Maureen did it and so did several of her classmates. I don't remember the menu entrees but I do remember that the diet was rather meager and somewhat unappealing with a fair amount of repetition. But it was nutritionally sound and would have been sufficient to sustain a family for a lifetime.

That assignment made a big impression on me. At the time I was spending about $100 per week on food. I decided then and there to cut that to $70 per week. Hey, if a family of four can have a sound diet on $25 per week, I should be able to feed my family of five quite well on $70. I could even save more if I had a big freezer, bought in bulk, or raised a garden but I don't do any of those things so I set out to save a modest $30 each week ($1560 every year).

After only 8 years, thanks to my saving and Bill's investing, we turned that idea into a little over $17,000. Since the early years, we have had one child leave home and we have boosted our food budget to $75 per week, but I'm happy to say that I've kept track of every penny spent on food and I'm still on target. Not only have I saved money; we actually eat better and healthier than before. Here are some things you can do to feed your family better on less:

- Make a menu for one week for all meals plus snacks. Then make a list of things to buy for that menu. Never step into a supermarket without a list. It gets you through the store in less than half the time and prevents impulse buying. It also saves time throughout the week: No more, "Let's see, what should we have for dinner tonight?" Prepare your menu and shopping list in the kitchen so you can check and see what you already have on hand. This prevents double buying and associated waste, especially with things that don't store long, like fresh produce.

- Go through the coupons from the Sunday paper and clip those that apply to your list. The coupons will more than cover the cost of the Sunday newspaper.

- Buy generic/house brand products when there is no quality difference. Examples include cereals, rolled oats, flour, sugar, oil, spices, butter, salt, tea, nuts, chocolate chips, and powdered milk (which I use for baking only).

- Avoid processed food like cookies. Bake your own using healthier ingredients. No TV dinners, frozen pizzas, or, gosh, I haven't bought that stuff in so long I can't even remember the junk I used to buy. Goes to show how much I miss it.

- Eat more turkey and less red meat. It's cheaper and healthier.
- Eat more fruits, vegetables, and grains.
- Switch to skim milk. Also healthier and cheaper.
- No alcohol. No lottery tickets.
- Never purchase nonfood items in a supermarket. Items such as shampoo, diapers, foil, and tissue are almost always cheaper elsewhere.
- Stretch food. I add an extra can of water to frozen orange juice along with a little sugar. It tastes more like fresh squeezed and I get more servings. Use your imagination.
- Get your calendar out as you make up your menu and plan the menu to fit your schedule. If you're taking Bobby to the orthodontist after school on Tuesday, plan a quick meal for that night. That way you won't be tempted to grab fast food on the way home.

Think, plan, and focus. The food-buying process is an area that can be improved in most homes but it won't just happen on its own. Think it through, make a plan, and stay focused as you implement your plan. You truly can eat better on less. Thanks, Maureen, for sharing your college assignment with me. It was a $17,000 (and counting) conversation. We're eating better and over the course of a lifetime we expect to save more than enough to buy a great house.

ENTERTAINMENT

Having Fun Without Breaking the Bank

We don't spend much on entertaining ourselves but that really wasn't something we chose to cut back on. It just happened. You see, Tim was born when we were in our early twenties. We'd only been out of college for a couple of years and like most recent college grads, we were pretty social. But Tim was quite ill. He'd have episodes of dangerously high blood pressure and we were just plain scared to leave him with a sitter, and most sitters were just as scared to care for him. We had only been married for a short time and we weren't about to live separate lives, with one of us going out and the other staying home. So we stayed home a lot. We never knew when we'd encounter a medical crisis or a middle of the night rush to the emergency room, so we had to stay alert. And sober. We couldn't, didn't, and still don't drink alcohol except for a rare glass of wine with dinner. But only one of us can have that glass of wine, even at home. One never knows when a medical crisis will strike. So, we're always ready.

If that sounds like a bleak existence to you, it's not. We're happy, content, and satisfied with life. You see, we've learned how to have fun and enjoy life in different ways. We didn't do it to save money, we did it because we had to, but now we like it that way. Oh, we do go out to eat fairly often, but we tend to hit pizza places and an occasional midrange restaurant like Ground Round or Carlos O'Kelly's. But many of the things we do for entertainment don't cost much. Here are a few examples:

Kids

- *Night games.* With all the organized sports and rec programs, kids are forgetting how to play. Remember those neighborhood night games we played when we were kids, like Hide-and-Seek and Capture the Flag? Our parents had to drag us into bed, didn't they? Whatever happened to those games? Come to think of it, when's the last time you saw kids set up a Kool-Aid stand, go on a scavenger hunt, or catch fireflies? We encourage those activities.

- *Circus setup.* When the circus comes to town, take some folding chairs and go out and watch them set up the tents and care for the animals. It's as much fun as the circus.

- *International cuisine.* Your child studies a country, prepares a report about the country and helps plan a menu and prepare a meal of the country's cuisine. During the meal, the child presents the report with a question-and-answer period. The whole family learns about other cultures with some interesting food to boot.

Family

- *Bonfire.* Build a bonfire in an old grill in the backyard, sit around the fire and roast hot dogs and marshmallows.

- *Library.* Public libraries sponsor many children's events like story hour, puppet shows, animal exhibits by park rangers, craft activities, and visiting authors.

- *Cabin on a lake.* For less than a thousand dollars a family can rent a nice cabin with a boat for a week.

Couples Only

- *Candlelight dinners.* No kids allowed. Get them a movie and banish them from the dining room. If they disturb you for anything but an emergency, they're in trouble. Cloth tablecloth, cloth napkins, candles, music, a great meal, and good conversation.

- *Dinner theater.* It's a windy, 20-below-zero Friday night in January. Our king-size bed is surrounded by candles. A tablecloth is spread on the bed, kind of like a picnic. A terrific meal is served on a big wooden platter while we watch a great movie. It doesn't get any better.

- *Midnight read-a-thons.* Go out on the screen porch or patio on a late summer night long after the kids are in bed. Settle into your comfy outdoor swivel rockers that are equipped with small book lights. Put your favorite drink and snacks on your side table and read a great book. Some of our favorite novelists are David Balducci, John Grisham, Ken Follett, Mary Higgins Clark, Michael Crichton, and Leon Uris. There's nothing quite like the late night air, night sounds, the quiet company, and the excitement of a super novel.

- *Board games.* We're real competitive and play to win.

We've learned to enjoy life even though we haven't been able to do some of the things other couples do on a regular basis, and we've saved a bundle in the process. Even though we're quite content, we're not suggesting that everyone should try to save money by dramatically reducing entertainment expenses. All we're saying is that it is possible to replace costly recreation with inexpensive or free activities, and you can do it without being miserable. If you go out every weekend and spend a hundred or so on drinks and dinner, it is possible to do it a different way and still be happy. Even very happy.

Impulse

How to Control Miscellaneous Spending

$3.86—Matching paper cups/plates with Christmas theme. *"Oh, how nice!"*

$1.79—Ice cream sundae. *"I'm starved!"*

$4.25—New shade of lipstick. *"That'll look good with my new red blouse."*

$6.85—Exfoliating scrub. *"Cool. I think I'll try it."*

$3.70—Two decorative bicycle license plates. *"A little something for the kids."*

$1.45—Sparkly nail polish. *"A little something more for the kids."*

$6.25—Coffee and roll on the way to work for me @ $1.25 per day for 5 days

$6.25—Ditto for Bill

$5.00—Two cans of pop per day at work @ $.50 per can for 5 days

$5.00—Ditto for Bill

$44.40 Subtotal

$ 2.22 Tax

$46.62—Grand Total for a Week

$2424—Grand Total for a Year

$19,392—Grand Total for 8 Years

$26,733—Grand Total if you invest $2424 per year and earn 9 percent for 8 years

---

Trinkets, baubles, treats, mementos, souvenirs, tokens. It's the little stuff that kills us, isn't it? Most of it is junk anyway so who needs it? But it isn't that easy to control these small impulse purchases. As we're walking through the discount store hundreds of things scream to be bought. "I work hard," we think. "I deserve this treat. And besides, it's only a couple bucks. Big deal!" But it is a big deal, isn't it? $26,733. Look again. $26,733. That's our estimate of what we have in the bank now because we stopped buying junk a few years ago. $26,733 in only 8 years. That's enough to cover the costs of all of these things for the rest of our lives:

- *Appliances:* refrigerators, washers, dryers, microwave ovens, TVs, VCRs, stoves, range hoods, dishwashers, garbage disposals, freezers
- *House maintenance:* roofs, concrete work, furnaces, central air, plumbing, electrical
- *Internet access*

That's right. It's enough to pay for all that for the rest of our lives. If the TV is shot, buy a new one. Need a new roof? No problem. Refrigerator on the blink? Get it fixed. E-mail; it's covered. We'll never need to work to pay for all those things again. It will all be paid for by the income off the money we *didn't spend* on trinkets for those 8 years. We're purchasing our future with junk. What a deal!

Getting a grip on impulse buying really matters and it has comprised an important part of our plan to achieve financial freedom. Because we've consciously changed the way we think about money, impulse buying isn't much of a problem for us anymore. It used to be, but it seems the more money we have, the less we buy on impulse. In the following paragraphs, we describe how we licked the problem.

Enthusiasm. We're on a mission to achieve self-sufficiency utilizing income from our assets and one part-time job between us. We'll soon eliminate full-time work from our lives. Forever. We'll have more time and will fill that time with activities we're enthusiastic about. Life will be easier, more enjoyable, more fulfilling. Ours is a life-changing mission of massive proportions. So every time we buy something on impulse, we feel badly because we know in our hearts we've delayed the achievement of our goal. And every time we resist the temptation to buy on impulse, we feel good because we've accelerated movement toward our goal. Our minds have been intentionally conditioned to resist impulsive buying. Resisting feels good.

Gratitude. Because we don't do much impulse buying, we tend to get a bigger "rush" from the things we do buy. Think about it. If you're buying a bunch of baubles and gadgets on a regular basis, they ultimately don't provide much pleasure because you're immersed in them. When you stop buying them, though, you'll feel pain. It's like an addiction. By reducing impulse buying you'll eventually increase your pleasure. Those occasional splurges will become treats again. You'll appreciate them. That's how we feel now.

Contentment. We are truly happy with what we have and don't feel the need for more. By following the strategies in Part One of this book, we've learned to enjoy life without buying those little "rewards" that are always so prominently displayed in the stores. We're content. We have enough.

Guilt. As long as there are people in the world who are hungry due to lack of food, cold due to lack of shelter, or sick due to lack of medicine, we feel obligated to help . . . to give. The least we can do is to divert money wasted on junk we don't need to people in crisis—to somebody's child, or mother, or father. Our faith demands that we help. So if we can cover some of our living expenses by reducing impulse buying, it frees up funds for charitable causes.

Impulse Buying Processor. Like many wives and mothers, I do most of the day-to-day buying for our family, so I'm the one enticed by all those little temptations as I stroll through the wares so skillfully displayed. These days, it's second nature to just pass by. But it hasn't always been easy. Actually, I'm a fairly easy mark for pretty displays and clever advertisements. I've never seen a sparkle or a glimmer that didn't catch my eye! I have particular weaknesses for things like holiday decorations, hot caramel milk shakes, french fries, earrings, barrettes and hair clips for my daughters, and souvenir tee shirts. For a long time my struggles with Madison Avenue always ended in defeat and victory: my defeat and their victory. I hate losing to advertisers, and so I fought back by developing what I call my "Impulse Buying Processor." Whenever I'm faced with an impulse buy, I base my decision on the following thought process:

1. Do I really need or want this?
   Yes. (Go on to question 2.)
   No. STOP. Don't buy anything. Examples: lottery tickets, those big orange pumpkin garbage bags for Halloween, a hard-boiled-egg slicer.

2. Can it wait?
   No. (Go on to question 3.)
   Yes. STOP. Wait awhile and repeat questions 1 and 2. Example: Wait on that milk shake until after my errands. Usually I either forget or run out of time.

3. Do I already own something similar that will suffice?
   No. (Go on to question 4.)
   Yes. STOP. Use what I already have. Example: Freeze individual slices of banana bread to take to the office instead of stopping for a donut.

4. Do I want this badly enough to delay progress toward our goal of achieving financial freedom?
   Yes. (Go on to question 5.)
   No. STOP. Don't buy it. It might be nice to have it but I don't want it bad enough to delay our goal.

5. Can I buy a similar but cheaper substitute?
   No. (Buy it.)
   Yes. Buy the cheaper substitute. Examples: large roll of white craft paper and colored ribbon instead of wrapping paper; postcards instead of envelopes, stationery, and stamps.

With practice, this thought process takes only seconds. It really helps to get me through the store without breaking the bank. But advertisers are tough to beat and they're continually coming up with new ways to entice me to buy those trinkets, baubles, treats, decorations, knickknacks, gadgets, and all those little things I love. Yes, I love them. But I love my freedom more.

I win.

Splurge

Coming Up for Air

Both of us were raised near lakes: Crystal Lake, Illinois, and Storm Lake, Iowa. So we spent a lot of time in the water and we liked to see how long we could swim under the surface without coming up for air. This was an important skill to develop for various kinds of stealth attacks on our peers. We could sneak up from quite a distance, but eventually we had to come up for air. Spending control is a little like holding your breath. We all need to come up for air now and then or we're likely to chuck the whole thing.

There are countless things you can do to control spending but some of them just aren't worth it. Here are some things we don't skimp on because it just isn't worth it:

- *Hot water.* If we want to take a 20-minute shower, we do.
- *Restaurant meals.* We don't go crazy, but eating out provides quite a bit of bang for the buck.
- *Vacations.* A lakeside cabin with a boat in northern Minnesota costs about a grand for a week. It's well worth it.
- *Maintenance.* On the house and cars.
- *School activities.* These are good experiences for kids at rock bottom prices.

- *Cable TV*. Everybody needs some quality flop time.
- *Air conditioning*. We refuse to sweat.
- *Heat in the winter*. We refuse to shiver.
- *Computer*. We have two and upgrade every 3 years.
- *Internet*. Access to the world at a reasonable price. E-mail brings families together again.
- *Decorator*. These folks are underused resources and they'll save you money in the long run.
- *VCR*. We have two.

It takes several years to accumulate enough to change your life, but you might not stick it out if you eliminate too much. You've got to come up for air now and then. Some savings enthusiasts recommend things like washing and reusing plastic bags and buying date-expired food. When we're asked if we plan to suggest things like that, we say, "Don't hold your breath."

PART FOUR

BIG TICKET
MONEY SAVERS

Taxes. Yikes! College financial aid. Help! It's really tempting to just bite the bullet and pay full freight on things that seem so terribly complicated and arcane. Sorry, but there's just too much money to be made by digging into the inner workings of some of these big ticket money savers. So put on your work boots, slip on your gloves, and get out the shovel. We're gonna do some serious diggin'.

RESEARCH

Money-Saving Strategies for Big Ticket Purchases

"Hi, Ed. Thanks for stopping. Come on down in the basement and I'll show you what I need. With the new furnace you put in last year, we really don't need the old brick chimney since the furnace is vented out the side of the house. We're putting on a new roof next week and the roofers will be knocking down the chimney. We don't know what to do with the gas water heater. It's vented through the roof now. What do you suggest?"

"Well, Bill, a lot of people are venting their water heaters out the side of the house. You could put in a heater with a power vent and seal off the roof entirely, or you could knock the brick chimney down and still vent the water heater through the roof. Initially, it would probably cost about the same either way if you don't count the cost of the new water heater which you probably will need soon anyway."

"What about long-term costs?"

"Well, that's what I was just getting to. If you buy a water heater with a power vent it will cost another $200 or thereabouts to replace it when it wears out."

"OK. Let's keep this water heater and vent it through the roof. That'll save money in several ways. First, I should be able to get a year or so of life out of my present heater. I'll also save a couple hundred bucks when I replace it in a year or two. And I'll continue to save every time I replace a heater for as long as I own the house."

"OK, Bill. Let me know when the roofers get to the chimney and I'll stop and vent this one through the roof."

"Great. See you then."

You know, it seems like we end up spending more every time we buy something without first researching our options. But the reverse is also true. Every time we examine our options, we spend less. Sometimes far less. Usually it doesn't take more time; it's often just a matter of asking a few questions, like we did in the discussion with our plumbing and heating contractor. We believe in examining all options before purchasing any product or service that costs more than $50 or involves regular ongoing payments (like telephone service). We have several thousand dollars now that we wouldn't have had without these efforts. Here are a few more examples:

We buy most of our computer hardware and software over the Internet. A few months ago we were looking for a CD-R/RW drive that would enable us to make our own compact disks (CDs). First, we selected a reliable drive by reading reviews of those drives on the web at ZD Net (http://www.zdnet.com/). After selecting a good drive, we posted our selection in a computer newsgroup, asking others in the group to make recommendations about that drive and others based on their personal experiences. Next, we checked prices at Price Watch (http://www.pricewatch.com/). A company we'd never heard of was offering the drive for about $60 less than the next lowest price. But because we'd never heard of that outfit we were reluctant to buy from them until they had been around awhile. So we E-mailed five large, well-established Internet computer stores, told them we could get the drive at a $60 discount, but preferred to do business with them, and would pay them $5.00 more than the cut-rate outfit. All responded. Two said they wouldn't negotiate. Three said they would and one of those accepted our offer. In about an hour we found the best product, bought it at a cut rate from a big, reputable company, and saved $55.

Sometimes we ride on the coattails of others. Last fall we noticed our neighbor was using a leaf blower to clean up in the fall. We'd been thinking about getting one so we went over and took a look at his. This man is well known in the neighborhood for researching before buying, so we simply took his advice and acted upon it. We couldn't find his exact model but we bought something similar.

In Iowa you can choose which elementary or high school your child attends. With college costs out of sight, choosing a good public or private school can mean a better education and more scholarship opportunities down the road. Of course, word of mouth is important in selecting a school, but it's also important to check out standardized test scores. Just call the school administrative offices and ask for the average for each grade. You can also visit the school and sit in on classes to get a glimpse of teaching styles and curriculums. And while we're on the subject of schools, why not choose a teacher for your child? We've done that. First, we check with friends who are teachers to get a couple of names. They know who is good. Then we simply call the principal and ask for one of those teachers. They've always granted our requests, and we've had some terrific teachers for our kids.

When we were children, we learned a bunch of gross stuff from our cousins. They'd ask something like, "Which would you rather do . . ." and then they'd give you two choices of totally gross things. God, we loved those guys! Choosing a long-distance telephone carrier reminds me of the choices offered by my cousins. Choose your poison. If only there were somewhere to go for help. Well, there is. Check out http://www.teleworth.com. There you'll find info on some of the best deals. Also check out "PK Communications" at http://pkcomm.com for a super rate calculator. All you do is select your state and an estimate of the time you'll spend calling both in and out of state. There's even an option to include international calls. It will direct you to the five best deals for you. Once you find the best deal, make the switch and then tell your local phone company *not* to change your long-distance carrier unless you tell them to do it *in writing*. That will protect you from "slamming," a tactic used by some phone companies to switch you to their higher rates without your permission.

For purchases of major appliances, electronics, and cars, there's no better source than good old *Consumer Reports* magazine. They are on your side. Every family should subscribe. Also check out a fabulous website created by Edgar Sworsky, who is a consumer advocate and lawyer. It's called "Consumer World" (http://www.consumerworld.org/) and it is absolutely loaded with links to some of the best consumer resources on the Internet. We use it frequently for all kinds of prepurchase research. There you'll find buying advice, product reviews, low rate credit cards, discount travel, mortgage rates, consumer rights, and much more.

Is your bank sticking you with high fees for things like ATMs and checking accounts? How about your bank's savings accounts and certificates of deposit (CDs)? Is the interest you're getting less than you're seeing elsewhere? If the answers to these questions are yes, it may be time to do a little digging into other options. First, check into credit unions in your area. They usually have better deals than banks. For savings rates, go to the Internet and check out "Bank Rate Monitor" (http://www.bankrate.com). There you'll see some of the country's highest advertised savings rates. Take that information to your local banker and offer to invest in a CD there if they'll give you the same rate. Mary and I don't invest in CDs but our parents do and they've negotiated higher returns using that strategy. My dad was able to get a rate even higher than the highest advertised rate in the country because his local bank needed the money. All it takes is a little research and the guts to go in and ask.

We're very careful about selecting physicians. We've found that the best source of information about doctors is other doctors. They know who's good and who's not, but it's sometimes hard to get them to tell you. We've asked friends and family who have physician friends to check for us. That's worked well. We've also asked doctors who they go to or take their kids to. Before you choose a physician, at least check to see if he or she is in trouble with the medical board in your state. You'll find this information at the web site of the Association of State Medical Board Executive Directors (http://www.docboard.org).

The only way to choose a plumber, carpenter, roofer, mechanic, cabinet maker, or electrician is to check around. We have three friends who are well connected with different crowds, so we ask them to check around for us, and they do. Usually the same names come up. We've had great luck with skilled craftsmen.

These are just a few of the things we examine before buying. We're slow to part with money and do so only after careful research. As a result, we have saved several thousand dollars and improved the quality of the goods and services we buy. It really doesn't take much time. In fact, we save more money per hour spent researching than we make at our jobs. Far more. Try it. It's the easiest money you'll ever make.

Scholarship

A Debt-Free College Education for $7000!

Are you afraid that the cost of a college education will bury your child under a mountain of debt or put you into the poorhouse? It doesn't need to be that way. We know because our daughter, Colleen, graduated from college with money in the bank and no debt whatsoever. We paid a grand total of $7000 for the entire four years. We did it without any student loans or financial aid based on need. Here's how:

We fostered an enjoyment of learning and an appreciation for academic achievement throughout Colleen's formative years. We read to Colleen almost every evening from an early age. We praised her achievements and talked about her school day around the dinner table. When she earned excellent grades on her report card she earned dinner out with Dad at a restaurant of her choice. This father/daughter tradition was started when she was in junior high. Her good grades in high school paid off. She attended Winona State University in Minnesota and because of her excellent high school grades she qualified for resident tuition rates plus a $2000 per year academic scholarship.

Colleen worked summers and 10–15 hours per week during her last two years of high school and four years in college. During high school she spent $10–$15 per week and saved the rest, so she had about $3000 in the bank when college started. She didn't work more than 15 hours per week in high school or college because we had seen studies suggesting that working more than that tends to hurt school performance. Working up to 10 or 15 hours actually tends to improve grades, however. Colleen found this to be consistent with her experience. Her work at the local Dairy Queen forced her to stay on top of her studies and avoid putting things off because she never knew when she'd be called in to work.

We toured several colleges with Colleen and by September of her senior year she submitted applications to her top five picks. By applying to several schools she was able to compare financial aid packages and choose the best deal.

Speaking of financial aid, the whole system is rather complex. You'll need to learn the basics so your child receives as much aid as possible. We read a terrific book on the subject, *Don't Miss Out: The Ambitious Student's Guide to Financial Aid*, by Anna J. Leider and Robert Leider (Octameron Assoc., $8.00). Remember, though, that your financial situation beginning on January 1 of your child's *junior year* in high school will have an impact on aid received in college. Universities examine assets and income of both student and parents and then provide aid accordingly, so don't wait until the last minute to learn how the system works.

Because public universities are typically less than half the cost of private colleges, we took a look at some state schools in our area. We found one that is only a 3-hour drive from our home, has a small-school atmosphere, and classes that are taught by professors, not teaching assistants (something to watch out for when checking into public universities). Colleen loved it and preferred it over all of the private schools she had seen.

Colleen graduated from college and is now attending graduate school. She was able to enter with no debt, so it will be possible for her to go all the way from high school graduation to a master's degree relying entirely on her part-time jobs, a scholarship earned by hard work in school, and only $7000 from her parents. Keep in mind that our $7000 and Colleen's work and scholarships covered *all* of her expenses such as tuition, fees, rent, utilities, food, clothing, books, supplies, and spending money. Sure, she was a good student, but even if she hadn't received a scholarship at Winona State, she could have accomplished the same thing with only about $15,000 from us if she had attended a public university in Iowa. So the next time you shudder at the thought of six-figure college bills, think again. There's a better way.

Oh, and one more thing. Colleen was about 12 years old when we made the agreement for those father/daughter dinners we mentioned at the beginning of this chapter, and we forgot to specify how long we'd do it. Well, Colleen has taken full advantage of that oversight and we're still buying dinners even though she has graduated from college. She says that she plans to collect her dinners all the way through graduate school, so we should probably add another several hundred for all these restaurant bills to the $7000!

TAXES

---

*Taking Advantage
of Tax Breaks*

Cutting your tax bill is both easy and difficult: easy in the sense that there is no self-denial involved, but difficult because you need to learn some of the intricacies of the tax code. To be fair, I'll 'fess up right now by acknowledging that I find tax preparation to be interesting. I actually kind of enjoy the tax preparation process. That's unusual, I know, but it helps us get through it. Mary despises everything about it. Unfortunately, she's better at it than I am. She can read the most cryptic instructions and make immediate sense out of them, so taxes are a team effort at our house. And that's good because both of us have a grasp of the big picture and as a result, we accumulated an extra $40,000. Roughly $40,000 in 8 years by cutting our tax bill and investing the savings. That's about $400 a month for 8 years! And that doesn't even count the money we saved by not paying taxes on the earnings of our retirement accounts. So as you can see, taxes matter.

Most families with children earning modest incomes fall into two tax categories: those who have enough mortgage interest to deduct and those who don't. You have the choice of taking what's called the *standard deduction*, which was $7100 for joint filers in 1998, or if you prefer, you can itemize your deductions. Simply add all possible deductions (things like deductible medical expenses, mortgage interest, etc.) and compare that to the standard deduction. Take whichever is larger. If you don't pay a hefty amount of interest on your house loan, you'll probably be better off taking the standard deduction. If you use the standard deduction, tax preparation is a breeze. Just order the federal and state instructions and do your own tax return. Don't waste your time running all over town to find tax forms and publications, just download what you need from the IRS at www.irs.ustreas.gov/. If you itemize, we suggest that you do two things. First, read *Taxes for Dummies* by Eric Tyson and David Silverman (IDG Books Worldwide, December 1998, $14.99). This book is an easy read and it will help you understand the tax process so you're sure to take advantage of every tax break available to you. Next, buy either Block Financial's Kiplinger TaxCut or Intuit's TurboTax. These computer tax prep programs walk you through an interview and perform all the calculations for you. Both are loaded with reference materials. Tax-saving opportunities are present throughout the year, so don't just hand over your taxes to a professional. If your mind is detached from the process, you're likely to miss out on some great opportunities.

The next best thing to lowering your tax bill is to defer taxes owed. One way to do that is to use retirement plans like individual retirement accounts (IRAs), 403(b)s, 401(k)s, SEPs, and SIMPLE IRAs.* You don't pay taxes on money put into these plans until you take it out, usually during retirement. Furthermore, your money compounds within those plans without incurring the drag of taxes, and that can really add up. Of course, you will pay taxes on those funds when you withdraw them later, but if you follow our path

---

*You've probably heard about 401(k)s and 403(b)s, which are employer sponsored retirement plans. You may not be familiar with SEP IRAs (Simplified Employee Pension plans) or SIMPLE IRAs (Savings Incentive Match Plan for Employees). They are also employer sponsored plans, but they're designed for small businesses.

and control your spending, your life will be very different then. You'll be working part-time at something you love doing but you probably won't be making as much as you're making now. Your needs and your taxable income will be greatly reduced and your taxes will probably be minimal, maybe even zero.

We put the maximum allowed by law into retirement plans, but most savers don't, probably because they're afraid they might need to use the money in an emergency. You see, if you take your money out of these plans before age 59½, you're slapped with a penalty and you're required to pay taxes on the withdrawal. Yikes. We think these fears are overblown, though. If you have sufficient insurance coverage for your house, car, health care, and disability, and if you have eliminated your debts and set aside 6 months to 1 year of living expenses, the chances of needing the money are slim. Still worried? Well, there is a solution to this dilemma. Save enough to max out any retirement plans you can get into, and still have enough left over to build a stash in taxable plans that you can access anytime you want. That's what we do. In just 8 years, we had assets totaling $264,000 in retirement plans, and $203,000 outside of them. So if we have an emergency, we can cover it without raiding our retirement accounts. If we can do that, so can many other families.

There is another way to postpone or defer taxes. If you invest in stock mutual funds outside of retirement plans, choose low turnover funds. Mutual funds are required to distribute, which means pass on to you, any dividends or capital gains they earn, and they must do that every year. They create capital gains by selling a security for more than they paid for it. So if you're investing in stock funds that aren't in retirement plans, it's important to choose a fund with a manager who considers tax consequences when he decides whether to sell or hold. Or better yet, choose a stock index fund like Vanguard's Total Stock Market Index Fund (1-800-871-3879). Index funds have minimal turnover.

If you are planning to buy shares of a mutual fund in an account that isn't a tax-deferred retirement account, don't do it shortly before the fund distributes a capital gain. Simply call the fund's toll-free number and say, "I want to buy your XYZ fund, but I want to wait if there's going to be a capital gain distribution within the next few weeks. When is the next distribution?" If it is coming soon, hold off on buying until that date has passed. If you don't, you'll owe taxes on a year's worth of gains after owning the fund for only a few days.

Most of the time Mary and I have managed to stay within the 15 percent federal tax bracket with occasional spillovers into 28 percent. If you're solidly within the 28 percent bracket, you might want to look into tax-free municipal bonds instead of CDs. With munis, you give up the federal insurance, but if you stick with highly rated bonds or mutual funds that invest in them, you'll almost always end up with more money in the bank. We've never owned them, but if we were in the 28 percent bracket or above, we would.

While we're on the subject of tax brackets, we'll make another confession. We used to think that if we moved to a higher tax bracket we'd be required to pay the higher rate on *all* of our taxable income. Here's how it really works. On a 1998 joint return, you'd pay 15 percent on the first $42,350 of *taxable* income. If you move up to the 28 percent bracket, you're not required to pay 28 percent on the first $42,350; you still pay only 15 percent on that. So if you're one of those people who passes up an opportunity to make some extra cash because you're afraid it will cost you more in extra taxes than you'd earn, relax. It always pays to earn more.

There's another widespread myth that never dies. Many believe that getting a big tax refund is good. It isn't. If you get a big refund, it means you've overpaid and given Uncle Sam an interest-free loan for a year or more. Getting a big tax refund is like paying double for your groceries every week for a year, and then filling out an application the following April asking the supermarket to send you a refund. What would you do if your grocery store said you had to do that from now on? Would you get all excited about getting a big grocery refund next spring? Well, getting a big tax refund is no different. It isn't a smart thing to do.

Mary and I work on the front lines in human services occupations. Every day we witness great things that are being done with our tax dollars so we don't resent the government or feel cheated when we send our tax check to the IRS or the State of Iowa. There is a tremendous amount of good, charitable, tax-funded work being done by competent, efficient, caring people in both the public and private sectors. Unfortunately, $200 toilet seats and $90 hammers make for exciting news. But you don't hear much about retarded people getting jobs, welfare recipients breaking out of the poverty cycle, or adults learning to read. We pay our taxes with the realization that much of it will be spent on very good things. But we also realize that the tax collection rules are written by a special-interest-driven political system that isn't looking out for the interests of families with children, so we aren't shy about using the few tax advantages that are there for us. We have more than $40,000 accumulated in only 8 years to show for it. So could you. Learning about taxes can be boring and painful. But $40,000 feels good. Real good.

PART FIVE

SIMPLIFY YOUR LIFE

We've all heard about antimatter while watching the adventures of Captain Kirk, Scotty, Mr. Spock, and the crew of the starship *Enterprise*. We have no clue what antimatter is, of course, all we know is this: If you mix antimatter with matter there will be trouble. Big trouble. Chaos and money are like matter and antimatter. They can't coexist and if you try to put them together, you'll end up with a mess. Driving out disorder creates an environment in which money will thrive. Here's how we defeated chaos.

SUPPLIES

Office Supplies You Must Have

I'm going to give you $1500. All you need to do is take two pieces of paper that are in your possession, make copies of them, and mail them to me. It will take about 15 minutes, so for time spent you'd be earning $6000 per hour. Would you do it? Of course you would? Well, don't be so sure. Part of my job is to provide grants to college students, both traditional students and adults. It's money that does not need to be paid back. All I need from the students are copies of two documents. But sometimes students don't drop those two pages into the mail, even if I send reminders. They just don't get it done.

Why does that happen? It isn't lack of intelligence. These people are earning college degrees. It isn't that they don't need the money. Most are seriously strapped for cash. Laziness? No way! Many of these folks are full-time students working part-time and sometimes even full-time minimum wage jobs. Yet a surprising number of these people will just walk away from $1500, a sum they'll work nearly 300 hours to earn. You heard it right. Some college students qualify to receive a $1500 grant to pay for some of their college expenses, but first they must send verification of other aid (to prevent an overaward), and sometimes they don't get around to doing it. They simply walk away from $1500. Why?

We suspect that people let things slide because they are disorganized, and they're disorganized because they don't have the "stuff" of organization—office supplies. If you don't have envelopes, stamps, files, calendars, organizers, or any of the other necessities, it's just too easy to set something aside until later. Problem is, the pile keeps growing, deadlines pass, bills aren't paid on time, opportunities are lost, and before long you're in a perpetually chaotic situation. Some folks even give up and resign themselves to a fate of permanent disorganization. They may joke about it and say things like, "Well, you know me, I'd forget my head if it weren't screwed on," or, "I guess that got lost in the shuffle, you know how that goes!" You're supposed to say, "Oh, I sure do . . . ha, ha, ha."

If your life is out of order, consider buying office supplies. Think about it for a moment; in some ways a family is like a business. There's money coming in that must be handled, sometimes even more money going out, appointments to keep, commitments to honor, insurance and other billing screw-ups to address, opportunities to pursue, and taxes—just like a business. Many families these days are holding down two jobs, raising children, maintaining a house, managing a portfolio, and continually upgrading work skills in order to survive in a rapidly evolving world economy. It's just too much to manage with a shoe box, a scratch pad, and a pencil. Here's a list of office supply "must haves":

- *Computer.* There's no better way to examine your spending habits or track your finances. You can buy a used system that will do that for less than $300.
- *Printer.* If you want to be taken seriously, type it and print it. Responding to an important letter? Print an extra copy for your records. You can buy a new printer for under $200.

- *File cabinets.* Still using an old shoe box? A light duty, metal, two-drawer filing cabinet will set you back about twenty bucks. Get two.

- *Manila folders.* You can get 250 of these for $10. Your new filing cabinets won't be much use without these.

- *Quicken.* In our opinion, this personal finance software is the best. You can buy the Deluxe version for $60 or get last year's version through an Internet auction like Ebay (http://www.ebay.com/) for less than $20. Actually, some of the older versions are just as good if not better in some respects.

- *Boxes with lids.* No, not the kind you get for free at the grocery store, the kind you buy in an office supply store. These come in handy for storing old records you're reluctant to toss, but are hogging space in your filing cabinets. They're sturdy, have snug-fitting lids, and are sized to hold either letter- or legal-size records. You can get five of the better quality storage boxes for $14.

- *Stamps.* You know, it might be really painful to pay $33 for a roll of 100 stamps but unless you do, you'll always be out of them when you really need them. You're gonna use 'em anyway, so buy them!

- *Paper.* Get a thousand sheets. It'll cost about $10.

- *Regular envelopes.* Five hundred of these will set you back $12.

- *Letter-size manila envelopes.* Buy 250 for about $16.

- *Scissors.* Purchase two for about $5 each.

- *Stapler.* A good one will run about $12.

- *Small stuff.* Rubber bands, staple remover, regular tape, packaging tape, pens of different colors, permanent markers, correction fluid, paper clips, and boxes of various sizes for shipping. All this will cost about $30.

Assuming you're starting with nothing, you can have all you need for about $700 and that includes a computer and a printer. The next time someone offers to give you $1500 for 15 minutes of your time, you'll be ready.

Your family is on the road to financial freedom, and that is a serious business. You owe it to yourself to treat it like one.

FILES

Building a Bulletproof Filing System

Most of us make to-do lists that consist of jobs that aren't too bad, jobs that are hard, and jobs that are just plain ugly. Ugly jobs. Those are the tasks that stay on our lists week after week. Designing a filing system is an ugly job but once it's done . . . well, you know you'll feel better.

A good record-keeping system has only one requirement. It must enable you to find whatever is in there quickly. We have had some terrible systems over the years but we finally nailed it down. Here's how it works.

In one drawer we have our "Owner's Manual Files." The drawer is filled with manila folders, each labeled with a letter of the alphabet. When we buy a television, we staple the receipt to the owner's manual and put it in the folder labeled **T**. All the durable goods we buy are in there, so if we need to learn how to change the air filter on the lawn mower, or collect on the warranty when the washing machine breaks, we grab it in a snap. Every few years we go through it and purge all the records on the things we no longer have.

The other drawers in our filing cabinets contain our main system. It's pretty simple. We start with manila folders, each labeled with a letter of the alphabet. If we want to save something, like maybe a map of the Amish area, we'd file that in the **A** folder because it is a one-page, one-of-a-kind item. We live near an Amish community and would use that map to find their bakery or woodshop. But you don't want your **A** folder to contain too much or it will be a chore to dig through, so for something like ancestor records that contain quite a few things (we are into family history), we'd label a separate manila folder "Ancestor Records" and keep it in the file cabinet drawer right behind the **A** folder.

When you build your filing system you don't want to have to get down on your knees and dig through files to find something. Avoid this problem by keeping a log of everything in the filing system. Here's how:

- When you're first putting your filing system together, sit on the floor with your spouse in front of your new filing cabinets and a pile of all your records. Plan to spend a full day.
- Label each of 26 pages of notebook paper with a letter of the alphabet.
- Start filing your pile, one page at a time. Let's take the Amish map. It's a one-page, one-time item so it doesn't need its own manila folder. Now ask each other this: When I want to find this Amish map in 10 years, what am I likely to look under? One of you might say "Amish" and the other "Map." Anything else? Well, maybe "Bakery" or "Woodshop." So we'll file it in the **A** folder but we'll cross-reference it under "Map," "Amish," "Bakery," and "Woodshop." To do that, follow these steps:

  Put the map in the **A** file.

  On your notebook page labeled **A**, write this:
  Amish—Map—Bakery—Woodshop . . . .**A**

On your notebook page labeled **B**, write this:
Bakery—Woodshop—Amish—Map . . . . **A**

On your notebook page labeled **M** write this:
Map—Amish—Bakery—Woodshop . . . . **A**

On your notebook page labeled **W** write this:
Woodshop—Amish—Bakery—Map . . . . **A**

Now, move on to the next item in your pile and follow the same routine until it's all filed. When you're done, gather those 26 pages of paper, type them as a log using a two-column format in your word processor, hit alphabetize, and print it. In the future, as you put new items into your system, add handwritten entries to your typed log in red ink and in a year or so, add the new entries to your word processing file and reprint a fresh log. Store your log in the front of your first filing cabinet in a brightly colored folder. When you need to find your Amish map, grab the log, look under "Bakery" or "Amish" or "Map" or "Woodshop" and it will shoot you to the **A** file. You'll never lose anything again.

We keep canceled checks and bank statements for 7 years. Mutual funds usually send a cumulative statement at year's end which we keep, especially retirement plan statements; we never throw those away. All we really need is a record of every single transaction. We also hang on to the most current fund prospectus and all correspondence we've generated with the fund companies, but we toss almost everything else they send. If we didn't, we'd eventually need a semi to haul it all away.

Some records are so important that it's a good idea to keep them in a fireproof box in the basement. Why the basement? If your house burns down you don't want your firebox to fall two stories onto a concrete floor. Don't take chances with things like tax returns, insurance records, and year-end retirement plan statements. We list these things and cross-reference them in our log along with everything else but note that they're in the firebox in the basement.

Building a good filing system isn't anyone's idea of a good time, but it only takes a day and once it's done you're set. You'll have quick, trouble-free access to records that will enable you to cash in on warranties, save on your taxes, or cover yourself on any number of things that can go wrong. Spend one day and do it right or spend a lifetime fumbling, digging, cussing, and losing out on opportunities to save money. It's an ugly job that pays. So, what are you doing next Saturday?

BATHROOM

Strategies That Keep a One Bathroom Home Running Smoothly

Housing is incredibly expensive, so anything you can do to keep those costs down will result in big payoffs over the long haul. One way to cut housing costs is to buy a one bathroom home. Many people would turn up their noses at a home like that. But how many years are you willing to keep your nose to the grindstone to pay for that extra bathroom? Five years? Three years? Two years? If you aren't willing to sacrifice a chunk of your life in exchange for that extra bathroom, we've got good news for you. It is possible for a family with children to survive in a one bathroom house. Actually, many of our parents and grandparents growing up during the 1920s and 1930s managed to survive with an outhouse and no indoor plumbing at all. Imagine bundling up to go out and use the outhouse when it's 20 below zero with a 50 mile per hour wind. Imagine how thrilled they'd have been to have indoor facilities with running water. Yet most families today wouldn't consider living with fewer than two bathrooms.

Getting by with one isn't a cakewalk but it can be done. All it takes is planning, organization, and a little cooperation. Here are a few strategies that have worked for us.

If you have five people clamoring to use one bathroom, some thoughtful scheduling will minimize the times that everybody needs to be in there at once. For example, schedule daily showers so that there is enough time and enough hot water for everyone to get showered every day. Some people prefer to shower at night, others in the morning. We've assigned time slots that everyone can live with. We've also adopted the "bladder first" rule. No one is allowed to take a shower or tie up the bathroom for any substantial length of time without first checking to see if anyone needs to use the bathroom first. If Dad has just polished off a two quart jug of iced tea and someone jumps into the shower, well, you get the idea.

It's important to design the bathroom for maximum efficiency. We placed the sink into a countertop that is about 6 feet long and installed a large mirror that runs the entire length of the countertop. Above the mirror we have a string of lights. This allows two or three people at a time to do hair and makeup because the lighting is bright and equally dispersed along the entire counter. We also put several hooks on the back of the bathroom door so there's plenty of space to hang wet towels. There's a powerful exhaust fan to prevent steam on the mirror so one girl can take a shower while another is fixing her hair.

We have a small closet in our bathroom that we filled with shelves to hold small plastic baskets. In one basket we keep all of our medical supplies. If you need to find some Tylenol, you don't have to dig through hairbrushes, toothpaste, and shampoo bottles to find it. We each have our own personal basket, too, which contains the things we use on a daily basis like a toothbrush, toothpaste, combs, floss, nail clippers, makeup, razor, deodorant, etc. When it's your turn in the bathroom, you just grab your basket and go to it. There's no digging or searching, so things move quickly. There is some initial cost because everyone has their own clippers, toothpaste, floss, hairbrush, and so forth, but it is well worth it in time saved.

Everyone is responsible for keeping track of their own supplies. We have a small erasable board attached to the back of the closet door with a felt tip marker attached to it. If someone is running low on toothpaste, she simply writes that on the board. When it is time to go to the store, it's a simple matter to list the things that are written there. Once again, it speeds things up, keeps things organized, and Mom isn't forced to dig through all the supplies to see what's running low. She just goes to the board and jots down what's needed.

We keep plenty of washcloths and towels on hand. This cuts down on the need to do laundry during the week. Washcloths are $3.96 a dozen so buying three or four dozen won't break the bank.

We have mirrors in all bedrooms and in the kitchen so there's always a place to fix hair and put on makeup if the bathroom is tied up. Of course, there is also the kitchen sink for a quick tooth brushing or face washing. Since we each have our own personal basket, we can just grab that out of the bathroom and get busy.

With a few simple strategies, a family can live in a home with one bathroom and survive to tell about it. It isn't luxurious living but it sure beats heating your bath water on a wood stove and climbing through snow banks to use the toilet in the middle of the night.

SLEEP

The Costs of Losing Sleep

There was an episode of *Seinfeld* a while back about a barking dog that kept Elaine from sleeping. Eventually, she hired Newman, the evil postal worker, to kidnap the dog. I can relate to that. Many years ago we had a neighbor who had three or four cars, none of them with working mufflers. He started one of those clunkers every day at about 5:00 A.M. Then he'd go into the house and let it warm up for about a half-hour or so. He had lots of visitors on weekends at all hours of the night, and most of them had worn out mufflers on their cars, too. That is probably the only time in my life that I have experienced pure rage. I don't know about you, but when I don't get enough sleep, I'm miserable. I can't function on my job, read a book, concentrate, or behave civilly. And I certainly can't focus on the intricacies of personal finance.

If you're having trouble getting sleep, you'll need to root out the causes and fix them. All kinds of things can rob you of sleep. Here are a few we've encountered:

Kids who won't go to bed. Most parents can visualize this scenario: Your 5-month-old is sucking down a bottle and falls asleep in your arms and you're thinking, "Thank God!" You get up very, very slowly and tiptoe toward the crib, being careful not to jostle the baby. Everything is going great as you approach the crib. The baby is hanging in your arms like a limp rag doll. You slowly lower her down into the crib while everyone else in the family holds their breath. The baby touches the mattress, her eyes pop open and she screams to the high heavens as if to say, "How dare you try to trick me like this!" When our youngest child, Meghann, was born, the hospital nurses provided some valuable advice we had never heard before: Never wait until the baby is asleep to put her in bed. Put her down when she is sleepy and keep a normal background noise level; no whispering or tiptoeing around. Well, it worked beautifully. Meghann learned to fall asleep without depending on Mom's warmth, Dad's rocking, and silence in the background.

What if you're already beyond that point and your little one howls at the sight of her bed? You'll probably need to use the old Dr. Spock routine. Make sure the baby's tummy is full, the diaper is changed, and she isn't ill or uncomfortable. Smile at her and tell her it's time for bed. Put her down, kiss her good-night, leave the room, and close the door. Make sure you can see her to ensure that she isn't caught or in any other type of danger (you may need to peek in through an outside window), but make sure she can't see you. Our oldest, Colleen, became a tyrant at bedtime, so when she was 10 months old we put her down and let her cry. It was tough. Our instincts told us to rescue her. We went outside and peeked in at her through the window of our apartment complex and she was fine. On the first night, she squalled for 20 minutes. On the second, 10 minutes. On the third night, she cried for about 1 minute and after that she never cried again. What a relief! I wonder what our neighbors thought we were doing at the window.

111

Children crying from nightmares. Can you picture this scene? You are sound asleep. It's about 1:00 A.M. You wake up to the sound of a 4-year-old who has burst into tears about 3 inches from your face. She's crying hysterically, babbling, and making no sense. Probably a bad dream. The easy solution is to simply scoop the child up into your bed. Both you and the child will fall asleep very quickly. Problem solved, right? No! Pull the child into your bed and she'll show up again, and again, and again. Although it is difficult to drag yourself out of bed in the middle of the night, you're going to be far better off in the long run if you take your little one by the hand, go to her bedroom, tuck her in, sit beside her and stroke her hair until she calms down, and then proceed back to your bed.

What about sick children? There's nothing more miserable than a young child with a high fever and dehydration from vomiting. Of course, this type of crisis never happens during the day; it's always in the middle of the night when you must work the next day. You've got to keep an eye on the fever and try to get a little fluid down but it must be done gradually to prevent vomiting. So, what do you do? If you don't have one, buy an electronic kitchen timer. They cost about $10. They are like stopwatches and can be set quickly to sound an alarm whenever you want. Forget trying to fumble with an alarm clock. You need to be alert to set them (is this set for A.M. or P.M.?) and they go off while you're setting them and wake up the sick child as well as everyone else in the house. Physicians learn to fall into a deep sleep very quickly, arise fully alert to deal with emergency situations, and then fall asleep again. As a parent, you can learn to do this, too, but you can't do it without one of those timers. Get one, you'll never regret it.

To catch up on sleep, pick a day each week to sleep in. We sleep until 10:00 or 11:00 A.M. every Saturday. Before we go to bed on Friday night we set out breakfast for the kids. We put milk and juice in small pitchers so the little children can manage. Fruit is prepared and cereal is ready to serve. We shut off the phone, turn down the volume on the answering machine, and sleep. If the kids get up before we do, they don't disturb us for anything that isn't an emergency. If they do, they know they'll be shot on sight. We live for Saturday morning.

Without enough sleep you'll lose your job, your spouse, or your sanity, so fix whatever it is that's keeping you awake, even if it involves hiring a postal worker like Newman to kidnap an obnoxious barking dog. Hmm . . . I wonder if he'd have helped me get rid of those clunkers my neighbor liked to warm up at 5:00 A.M.?

PART SIX

PRACTICAL MONEY-SAVING SKILLS

Sometimes there's money lying around and all you need to do is reach down and pick it up. Easy money; that's what we call it, and there's a lot of it out there if you know how to find it. Oh sure, maybe it will involve a little time and know-how, but compared to rolling out of a warm bed at 6:00 A.M. when it's 20 below zero and dark outside, this stuff is a breeze.

REFUNDS

Recouping Your Money on Shoddy Work, Products, or Insurance Denials

Dear Mr. Toohey:

I'm responding to the letter you directed to (name of chief executive officer). I appreciate your frankness and extend an apology for the service hassles you have encountered.

A clerical error was made that caused your son's claim to deny. Steps are being taken to ensure that this problem does not occur again to you or other members. In the interim, the claim has been adjusted and payment was sent to the hospital on (date).

You are a valued customer, and I would be happy to offer my services to you. You may contact me directly on any future claims questions you may have. My telephone number is _____.

Sincerely,

(name)

Director

This is a real letter with names and dates redacted. In fact, it was a $700 letter, but it didn't come easily. It took six or seven letters and a few hours of our time, but it was worth it. I don't know about you, but our family can't afford to be ripped off by wrongful denials of insurance claims, shoddy services, or defective products, so we fight. We fight for the money, which has amounted to several thousand dollars over the years, but sometimes we also fight for principle. Large, wealthy, powerful companies shouldn't bully little people but sometimes they do. Unless we draw a line in the sand, working families who follow the rules and struggle to stay afloat will end up paying for products that don't work, services that aren't delivered, and medical expenses that insurance companies should be paying. Families shouldn't have to do that. In the end they'll just be paying for some executive's yacht, so, it's not just about money; sometimes, it's about fairness, too.

Most of the time goods and services meet or exceed expectations, and when they fall far short, it's usually simple to resolve. Most companies want satisfied customers and they'll make it right. But sometimes there's a showdown. Here's a few we've encountered:

- An orthodontist removed our child's braces prematurely and suggested putting them back on and charging several hundred dollars more to correct the mistake. But we had already paid him to complete the job. We negotiated and he refunded several hundred dollars. The next time we needed orthodontia we found a good dentist who agreed to do the job for significantly less than orthodontists were charging at the time, and his work was superb.

- A large financial company made errors on our statements, which exposed us to future difficulties with the IRS, but hey, anybody can make a mistake, so all we wanted was a correction. The staff were so rude and arrogant that their behavior became the issue, so in the end, they not only fixed the problem, they also gave us $150 in cash and some free services, and changed their system so it wouldn't happen to others.

- A medical supply company messed up our bill. It was one of those situations in which everything that could go wrong, did. In the end we got a call from their corporate attorney, a very nice fellow, who resolved the matter in one brief phone call. He even reimbursed us for our time and hassle. He assured us that systems would be reviewed to prevent similar problems in the future.

- We've received refunds or replacements on defective tires, paint, exhaust systems, patio furniture, even underwear. Believe it or not, I once had a package of underwear with the flies sewn shut! I didn't realize it until I was standing at a urinal several hours later. I thought I must have put them on backwards. I'm still reeling from that one.

So what's the best approach to resolve these disputes? Here are some things we've found helpful:

- *Be right.* That's the only power you've got. When you're right, you can overcome the resistance of the biggest, most intransigent opponents.

- *Write, don't call.* If you call, you'll get some clerk with no authority who will usually deny your request because she doesn't have the authority to grant it. Write to the store manager, company chief executive officer (CEO), or resident bigwig. Usually, you won't get a response, but that's good because it gives you an opening to write again, and now you have two grievances: the problem that caused you to write in the first place, and the discourtesy of ignoring your first letter. Make sure you enclose a copy of your first letter. It shows that you're "keeping track." This usually gets a resolution.

- *Keep copies of all correspondence.* Make a written summary of phone conversations.

- *Choose your battles.* Don't hassle over small items or gray areas. It isn't worth it. If it's not a black-and-white issue involving significant cash or important principles, forget it. Life's too short.

- *Keep it short.* In your complaint letter, do your best not to exceed one page. If you drone on at great length you won't be taken seriously.

- *Leave little guys alone.* We had a car stereo installed many years ago by a young man who botched the job. We paid him then took the car to someone else to fix it. If a waitress screws up an order, we usually ignore it. We get only one chance on this Earth and the time we're given is too limited to fill with regrets.

- *Be quiet.* If you're handling a dispute by phone, present your preferred resolution and then shut up. Most people can't stand silence on the phone so they'll fill the silence. Sometimes they'll agree to your proposal just to get off the phone with you.

- *Pass it on to a supervisor.* In your letter of complaint, if you aren't writing to the CEO, ask the person you're communicating with to share your letter with their administration. Point out that you're quite concerned about the manner in which your problem has been handled and you want to be sure managers are aware of the problem. Most employees won't want their bosses to know about problems like yours, but they'll also be reluctant to ignore your specific request for management's involvement. It might be easier to just give you what you want.

- *Provide deadlines and consequences.* "If this matter isn't resolved by (date), I will plan to (action)." In other words, take them to the edge of the cliff and show them how far down the fall will be.

- *Contain the damage.* If you're unfortunate enough to get into a dispute with a physician, try to contain the damage. Your medical records are confidential. Send a letter by certified mail requesting a copy of all medical records and include a statement in your letter that retracts any prior permission you may have provided to release your records. In other words, cut him off so he doesn't trash your reputation with other physicians. It's rare, but it happens, so act fast.

We've saved thousands over the years by fighting erroneous insurance denials and seeking refunds on defective products and services—at least enough to pay for one child's college education. And don't forget, every time you stand up and fight for what's right, you make things better for the rest of us. It isn't just the money. So, it's your choice. You can buy an education for your child or help to pay for some executive's yacht. I'll bet that's the easiest decision you've ever made. So get out there and stand up for yourself. It's time to kick some serious butt!

MAINTENANCE

Make Your Things Last Forever

Our things last forever. I mean it. We almost never have break-downs because we maintain our stuff. Proper maintenance increases the life of our home, cars, and appliances and decreases the amount of energy they use, resulting in significant savings over time. The key to maintaining your possessions is having a system to make sure it gets done. Actually, we have two systems, one for our car and one for everything else. The one for "everything else" is just a sheet of paper taped to the inside of a kitchen cupboard door and it looks something like the sample shown on the next page.

Other things listed on that sheet are air conditioner, furnace, water heater, lawn mower, range hood, and computers. All those items require regular maintenance. Even computers? You bet. Have you ever looked inside the case? There are dust bunnies in there! When is the last time you defragmented your hard disk? How about scandisk? Most of your equipment requires some simple maintenance. Simply check the list every 3 months and take care of the things that are due. Here are three more things you need to do:

1. Whenever you buy a new appliance, read the owner's manual, then file it so you can refer to it when maintenance is due. If the new appliance isn't on your maintenance list, put it there.

2. Keep a good repair/maintenance reference book or CD-ROM on hand for things that aren't covered in owner's manuals. Your local home supply store is a good place to find such a reference. We picked up a CD-ROM for about $25.

3. Improve your skills by watching Discovery Channel shows like *Home Matters* and *Gimme Shelter* or public TV shows like *Home Time*.

Car maintenance requires its own system. If you're like most people, you probably drive about 12,000 miles per year so you'll need to deal with car maintenance in January, April, July, and October. We only do a few simple checks (maybe 20 minutes total) in January and July. The example on page 124 shows what our system looks like.

From your car manual simply list each recommended maintenance item in the left column and put an X under the due date for each task. When the task is done, record the date of completion and

Sample Maintenance Schedule

Dates Maintenance Is Due				
Refrigerator	January	April	July	October
Dehumidifier			July	
House Roof		April		
Gutters		April		October
Clothes Dryer			July	
Bikes		April		
Deck/Porch		April		

Sample Car Maintenance Record

1988 Nissan Sentra	4/99	Date Done Miles	7/99	Date Done Miles	10/99	Date Done Miles
Change Oil	X	4/15/99 253,521			X	
Change Oil Filter	X	4/15/99 253,521			X	
Change Air Cleaner Filter	X	4/15/99 253,521				
Replace PCV Filter	X	4/15/99 253,521				
Inspect Belts	X	4/15/99 253,521	X	7/8/99 255,403	X	
Replace Belts					X	

the number of miles on the odometer. If possible, do some of the service yourself. For example, we change our oil and oil filter but we let our mechanic change our fuel filter. Put all the things your mechanic needs to do in the April column and when April rolls around, make a separate list for him. If your car is still under warranty, ask your mechanic to sign the list you provided so you'll have proof of service in case there is ever a warranty dispute. If you're doing the work yourself, keep receipts. If it is OK with your mechanic, you might also consider buying some of the supplies (spark plugs, belts, etc.) at a discount store so he doesn't need to run for them. You might save a few bucks and get your car back sooner.

In case you noticed, we don't really have 253,521 miles on our Sentra but if we stay on top of its maintenance we might make it. Besides, Bill cut a deal with a big repair chain that tried to pull a fast one on us (It's a long story). When all was said and done, they promised to replace the exhaust system for the life of the car, so Bill plans to keep that car alive forever.

Maintenance jobs are easy to ignore. There are always a million things you'd rather be doing. We've found that it helps to do most of these tasks in early April. After a brutal Iowa winter, it's a big novelty to be out in the fresh air in April. It also helps to:

- Block off a couple of weekends and get everything done fast so you can forget about it for the rest of the year.
- Work together. At least you'll have some pleasant conversation to keep you going.
- Have a radio on in the background. Well, on second thought, maybe that's not such a hot idea. Bill will probably want talk radio and I'll want music. So much for the pleasant conversation!

Taking care of our possessions contributes to financial freedom by prolonging their use, preventing costly repairs, and conserving energy. Staying on top of maintenance also improves the quality of our lives because everything will function safely and look better. So, get out those owner's manuals and start making lists. It's money in the bank.

SKILLS

Do It Yourself and Save

Sometimes it pays to do it yourself; sometimes it doesn't. A few years ago, a friend drove to our home in Iowa from about 4 hours away. From our house we took his car to Dubuque for a visit to our alma mater. That's about 1 hour away. When we got to Dubuque, the oil light flashed bright red. So we stopped and checked the oil. Nothing on the dipstick. Added a quart. Still nothing. So we kept adding, and adding, and adding. When we were done, we figured that he had been driving that car for 5 hours with only a little over one quart of oil in the crankcase! He had recently patronized one of those quick oil change shops. They drained the old oil, replaced the oil plug, and changed the oil filter. But they forgot to replace the oil. There was enough of the old oil left in the engine to keep him going for awhile but the engine probably got about 5 years worth of wear that day.

There are two reasons to do some things yourself. The first and most obvious reason is to save money. I change the oil on my two cars twice a year on average and I do it myself. I probably save a total of about $60 a year. Not much. But it isn't always about saving the few bucks you'd pay the professional to do it. No, sometimes it's really about making sure it gets done right. You care. Sometimes the pros don't.

Here are a few things we've learned to do ourselves over the years. By honing these skills we've saved a bundle, prevented countless headaches, and improved the quality of our lives.

Tax Returns. Most families have tax returns that are a breeze to complete. With all the tax prep books and software available, there's no need to hire a lawyer or an accountant to prepare your return. Besides, you can't afford to "disconnect" your mind from the tax collection process because the things you do throughout the year determine the taxes you'll pay in April. It's important to keep your head in the game and your eyes peeled for tax savings throughout the year. If you don't, all you're really doing is hiring an accountant to pay a bill that would have been much smaller with a little tax planning. Besides, if you don't know the system, you'll probably mess up and give your accountant inadequate or erroneous information. Also, keep in mind that tax returns are frequently botched by the pros.

Financial Planning. The financial services industry is riddled with conflicts of interest. Can you really afford to part with 5 percent of all the money you'll ever save to pay for the services of a planner or broker?

Job Placement/Resume Services. We've known people out of work and strapped for cash who forked over their last $500 to a placement agency. These were desperate people and all they received for their money was a basic cookbook resume on fancy paper. In the end, they found their own jobs. Anyone who thinks they may need to find a job someday (like everyone!) should read *What Color Is Your Parachute?* by Richard Bolles ($16.95, Ten Speed Press) and *Knock 'Em Dead* by Martin Yate ($12.95, Adams Pub). Don't wait until you're out of work. Do it now so you're ready with a plan when unemployment strikes you down.

Medical Care. With health-care costs skyrocketing, it behooves us all to learn something about health and medicine so we can keep ourselves well, handle our minor ailments without accessing the health-care system unnecessarily, and become helpful, cooperative, and active participants with our physicians. It's a matter of health and money. In our family, Mary shops for food and prepares our meals and as a part of that, she has studied nutrition in an effort to improve our wellness. We have medical and drug reference books on hand. One of our favorites is *How to Be Your Own Doctor (Sometimes)* by Keith W. Sehnert, M.D. (Grosset & Dunlap, 1975) which, unfortunately, is out of print, but there are plenty of other good references available. We've also benefited from the medical (although not necessarily the child-rearing) advice of Dr. Benjamin Spock's classic, *Dr. Spock's Baby and Child Care* ($6.39, Pocket Books, June 1998). Little kids get a ton of ear infections so we purchased an otoscope (that thing they look in your ears with) and asked our pediatrician to show us how to use it. He was glad to do it. Now we can spot an ear infection in the early stages and get treatment started quickly, before it gets out of hand. The quality of medical care our family has received has been significantly enhanced by our self-education. We've learned about communicating better with our physicians, avoiding unnecessary medical tests, asking good questions, and the importance of following instructions explicitly. These skills have put cash in our pockets and have improved the quality of our lives.

Computers. Many families still haven't jumped on the home computer bandwagon. If you're one of them, we'd suggest taking the plunge. We have two computers that we use to track expenditures, monitor investments, shop, complete homework assignments, play games, write letters, and, of course, we use E-mail, that wonderful technology that brings far-flung families together again. A computer will plug your family into limitless information on the Internet, information that will solve real problems. For example, Mary's brother, Mike, moved from the United States to the Philippines to work as a professor in a university there. When Mike was tragically killed in a plane crash, Mary was able to follow the crash and its aftermath by reading Philippine newspapers on the Internet.

Besides getting information about the crash that was so desperately needed, she noticed a comment in an article that said the airline was providing free tickets to Filipino families to attend the funerals. We contacted our Senator, the State Department, and airline officials in the Philippines (using E-mail) and obtained tickets for Mary and two other family members. We saved over $1200 per ticket on that transaction, and were able to handle all of those arrangements from our home.

In addition to being useful for research, the Internet has introduced a whole new way to enhance your quality of life. We preview movies, books, and music CDs over the Internet before we buy them. You can actually listen to CD music clips before placing your order. Several websites also recommend other musical artists or authors based on those you like. We've found some great books and CDs that way. What about weather reports before long trips? It's easy to get detailed reports from your location, but what about your destination? It takes only seconds on the Internet. Let's face it, many jobs already require computer literacy and it's probably only a matter of time until yours does. So, why wait?

Household Repair. Can you unclog a drain? Do you know how to maintain your computer using scandisk or defrag? How about replacing worn-out gaskets in a leaky faucet? Can you fix a hole in drywall, install a new telephone, or run a phone line to your computer? If you wanted to screen in your carport and make one wall removable so you could put your car there in the winter, could you build it yourself? Those are some things we've learned to do. If all of that sounds foreign to you, it's probably because you don't have a good instruction manual. We'd suggest *The Readers Digest New Complete Do-It-Yourself Manual* ($30.00, Readers Digest).

Health Insurance. You never know when a medical catastrophe will strike but if it does, it's crucial to have good medical insurance in place. But just having it isn't enough. You also need to understand your coverage so you don't do something that lets your insurance company shift its costs to you. Health-care reform in the United States has been badly bungled by our politicians and it remains, in our opinion, the most serious impediment to achieving financial freedom. Until health care is available to all, it will pay to maintain vigilance as systematic changes evolve, and review your current coverage so you can challenge insurance company denials and defend your position intelligently. Georgetown University has a superb website that describes your rights under legislation introduced by Senators Ted Kennedy and Nancy Kassebaum as well as individual state legislation (www.georgetown.edu/research/ihcrp/hipaa/). Take a few minutes to become familiar with your rights and review your current policy. If you're choosing coverage, we'd suggest that you consider this:

- First, make sure you don't choose a policy that excludes coverage for things you are likely to need. Get comprehensive hospital, medical, and drug coverage.

- Avoid HMOs if you can. You don't want to get into a position where the person providing or authorizing your medical care will lose money if you access a specialist or expensive technology. There is no conflict of interest more dangerous.

- Pay close attention to the policy's out-of-pocket maximum. That's the max you'll spend in a year in a worst-case scenario. And trust us on this, worst-case scenarios do happen.

- Watch out for lifetime maximum benefits. If you buy a policy with a lifetime maximum of a million, for example, the company can stop paying after they've spent a million. You don't want that if you can avoid it.

Car Maintenance. Get your car's manual out of the glove box, turn to the maintenance section, and make a list of things you can do yourself. Then stop in at an auto supply store and order or buy a repair/maintenance book written specifically for your car. While you're there, if you plan to change your oil, buy a steel oil filter wrench that fits the oil filter for your car. You'll probably save a few dollars by doing some car maintenance yourself, but more importantly, you'll do it right.

We've saved thousands of dollars over the years by honing our skills and doing things ourselves and you can, too. So if your oil light is flashing, you're in trouble with the IRS, you think "www" means World Wide Wrestling, and you're showering with your feet in 6 inches of water, consider improving your skills.

COMMISSIONS

Avoiding Sales Commissions and Insurance Company Financial Products

A few years back, a fellow we know got all hepped up about investing and attended a night class at the local community college. The teacher was a broker. Our friend assumed that the community college had given this broker its stamp of approval and the fellow really talked a good game, so our friend made an appointment to meet with him after the classes were finished. During that meeting he plunked down a big chunk of his life savings to buy shares in a limited partnership. At the time, limited partnerships were considered to be bad investments, but brokers were rewarded with big sales commissions for selling them. Our friend lost most of his investment.

At about the same time, another friend asked for help with her investments. She stopped by with a whole bundle of insurance company annuities. Most had performed very poorly relative to her other investments and she had a bunch of tiny annuities that were a nightmare to keep track of. She wanted to dump them and consolidate her portfolio into a manageable collection of five or six holdings that were likely to provide better returns. But she couldn't. The insurance companies wouldn't allow her to move her money without clobbering her with huge penalties. It makes sense, though, doesn't it? You're a large insurance company and you have a big sales force peddling financial products that most knowledgeable investors wouldn't buy. Eventually your customers may learn that they've bought an inferior product so what do you do? You hit them with big penalties if they try to move their money.

Rather than approach this subject diplomatically, we'll tell you exactly what we tell friends and family when asked about insurance company annuities and mutual funds that charge sales commissions. Here's what we say: "Don't buy them. It's stupid." Why? If you're paying sales commissions to a broker or insurance company, you're probably doing it for the financial advice because you don't know what you're doing. But, brokers and insurance company representatives are salesmen. You may get lousy advice.

Sales commissions on financial products are costly. Let's say you invest $1000 per month for 20 years and pay a 6 percent commission. That's $60 a month for sales commissions and in 20 years you're out $14,400. What are you getting in return? Now here's the part most of us forget. Although it would be painful to lose that $14,400, what really hurts is the loss of all the money you could have earned over a lifetime if you had invested the money wasted on sales commissions.

If you had invested that money in a fund that returned 10 percent on average, at the end of 20 years you'd have more than $45,000. If you were to retire then and leave that money invested for another 20 years you'd end up with more than $300,000. Granted, inflation would have eroded the value of the $300,000, but it would be worth about $88,000 in today's purchasing power (assuming 4 percent inflation) and that's too much to pay a salesman.

If a mutual fund doesn't charge sales commissions, how do they make their money? Simple. By charging hidden fees to cover the costs of managing your money, sending out statements, fielding your phone calls, and other things. All mutual funds have those annual fees (referred to as an "annual expense ratio") and they can run from about two-tenths of 1 percent of the amount you have in the fund up to 2 percent or more per year. But, some companies also hire a sales force and charge sales commissions *in addition to* the annual expense ratio. The mutual funds that don't charge sales commissions are called *no-load funds* and those are the only ones you should be using.

When it comes to insurance companies, there are lots of things you should be buying from them but investments isn't one. You probably need term life insurance, car insurance, home owners' insurance, and medical insurance, but don't buy investments from insurance companies. They charge some of the highest fees in the business. Some life insurance policies set aside part of the premium you pay and it builds up over the years, kind of like a savings account. Although it sounds good, don't buy it. The earnings on these investments are usually poor due to high expenses. You'll do better investing your money elsewhere. Just buy pure insurance that doesn't have a savings or investment component. I know, terms like *cash value, universal life*, and *whole life* sound good. But they're usually crummy deals. Remember: Insurance is insurance and investments are investments. Buy your insurance from one company and put your investments with another. Don't mix them!

Close your eyes and repeat five times:

> It is stupid to pay sales commissions on financial products.
> It is stupid to pay sales commissions on financial products.
> It is stupid to pay sales commissions on financial products.
> It is stupid to pay sales commissions on financial products.
> It is stupid to pay sales commissions on financial products.

Now say this five times:

> A broker is a salesman.
> A broker is a salesman.
> A broker is a salesman.

A broker is a salesman.
A broker is a salesman.

Now this:

Don't mix insurance and investments.
Don't mix insurance and investments.
Don't mix insurance and investments.
Don't mix insurance and investments.
Don't mix insurance and investments.

Repeat those three statements for as long as it takes to ensure that you won't pay sales commissions on financial products or purchase investments through insurance companies. If you can avoid that, you'll save a lot of money over the course of your lifetime, and it will be some of the easiest money you have ever made.

PART SEVEN

BE YOUR OWN
FINANCIAL EXPERT

People in their right minds would never perform complicated medical procedures on themselves or their loved ones. It's simply too complex and best left to trained physicians who know what they're doing. But, in our opinion, the same logic does not apply to financial matters. You're likely to do better if you learn the ropes and become your own financial expert. Why? Because the world of personal financial services is loaded with costly conflicts of interest, because nobody in this world cares more about your financial well-being than you do, and unlike medicine, personal finance really isn't all that difficult to learn. So should you do it yourself? You bet. Here's how to get started.

PLANNERS

The Best Financial Planner for You Is You

In 1990 we went shopping for a financial planner and met with three. Planner number one was a stereotypical salesman, and probably a good one, if such things can be judged by outward appearances like his beautiful plush office, expensive suit, and fancy car. We didn't know it at the time, of course, but he was pushing the highest commission mutual funds known to man and we almost bought what he was selling. Fortunately, he made two mistakes that scared us off. He told us that we couldn't lose money in his stock mutual funds unless "the world came to an end." Even neophytes like us knew that was nonsense. Then he did something very odd. When we asked for literature he pulled out a prospectus (booklet describing costs, risks, etc.) and he tore some pages out before handing it to us. Really! Right there in front of us he ripped them out. Forget this guy!

Planner number two was a nice fellow but when we told him how much we had to invest (about $20,000 at the time) he quickly lost interest. He mumbled something about maybe investing in treasuries or CDs and the meeting ended rather abruptly. Later we realized that he wasn't interested because we wouldn't generate enough commissions to make us worth his time.

Planner number three prepared a fancy computer generated book about us with all kinds of projections and a "plan" that called for us to save only about $4000 per year to be invested in a universal life insurance plan he was peddling. If we had followed his advice we'd have almost nothing today.

After meeting with these three we gave up on brokers and planners and set out to learn how to save and invest as much as possible, and how to do it in a hurry.

If you want to shift your fiscal life into high gear, one of the most important moves you can make is to become your own financial planner. Here's why:

- Buying investments through a broker or planner is expensive. For example, if you purchase mutual funds through a broker you'll likely be charged sales commissions of around 5 percent of the amount you invest. In other words, if you invest $10,000, the broker might receive $500 and you're left with only $9500. Ouch! Even more painful than the loss of $500 is all the money that the $500 could have earned over the course of your lifetime. Fortunately there are many good mutual fund companies that don't charge sales commissions. Two of our favorites are the Vanguard Financial Group and USAA.

- There is not a person in the world who cares more about your financial well-being than you. If you're looking for a financial planner without any conflict of interest, look no further than yourself.

- You should never invest in something that you don't understand. That is a basic rule of personal finance that you shouldn't violate because if you do, you'll be exposed to fraud or, more likely, you'll waste money on high-cost financial products that you'd never buy if you knew what you were doing. So you see, there is no getting around it. You need to learn the ropes.

- Financial planning encompasses a great deal more than just choosing investments. It involves psychology (how much risk is right for you?), relationships (how much should *we* save?), organizational skills (tracking expenses, record keeping, discipline), soul searching (what do you want out of life?), and spending habits (how will you control your spending so there is something left to save?). You are the only person who can address those crucial issues.

- Learning to manage your money isn't difficult. When we decided to do it we took a week of vacation and checked out a pile of books at the library. That provided us with enough information to get started. We'll list some of those books in the chapter entitled Homework.

OK, so you've decided to learn about personal finance and to develop your own financial plan but maybe you're a little leery of implementing it without some help. Relax. You don't need to tackle the job alone. When we were getting started, we prepared a written description of what we planned to do with our money and took it to an accountant who had some expertise in personal finance and tax matters. For a very small fee ($35), he made some good suggestions. More importantly, he provided some assurance as a neutral third party that we weren't making any major mistakes.

Deciding to be our own financial planners opened our minds to new possibilities that changed our lives. Don't put it off any longer. Do some soul searching, educate yourself, and implement a plan that is right for you. You'll never regret it.

FOUNDATION

Building Your Financial Future on Solid Footing

After speaking engagements, people come up to us and ask questions. All of them are highly motivated to achieve financial freedom but many tend to equate financial success with investing skills. They assume that their most important act will be choosing the right investments. When we try to change the focus to other more important issues, we usually encounter glazed and disappointed expressions that seem to say, "Yeah, yeah, I know all that, but what mutual fund should I buy?" Mary and I have toyed around with the idea of bringing my "little" brother Joe, a 30-year-old mountain, to our next speaking engagement so he can put some of these folks in a headlock and give them a dutch rub. If you have no older brothers you might not know that a dutch rub is where someone rubs the top of your head with his knuckles real hard and you go, "Ow! ow! ow!". While Joe was doing that we'd point to them and say, "Here's what happens if you ignore or minimize important steps on the road to independence." Actually, Mary hasn't really toyed with this idea other than to roll her eyes and tell me to shut up when I suggest it; but I still think it would be a great learning tool.

So let's get this out of the way now. *Investment expertise is one of the least important steps along the road to financial freedom for average families.* Yes, there are some things you need to know to avoid getting ripped off, and there are some bad investments you'll want to avoid, but it won't do you any good to know how to invest if you aren't ready to invest. This chapter is about some important matters that must be attended to before you are ready to invest. We call it "building a foundation" and here's a list of what you need to do:

- First, make sure that you have a decent education. If you're earning $7 per hour at a meat-packing plant, rescue yourself through education. Get a career, not a job. Unskilled workers in the United States are competing with workers in undeveloped countries now and you can't win that race to the bottom of the pay scale. Well, it is possible to win, I guess, but if you win, you lose. Get a skill!

- Save enough money to live on for 6 to 12 months. Plan to save at least $20,000 for this. If you don't, you'll lose your job in the next recession and you'll cash in your investments to live on at a time the investments have taken a hit, too. Besides, if you have $20,000 you won't be forced to take the first job that comes along.

- Pay off debt. It is idiotic to invest your money at 10 percent or so while having credit card debt at 17 percent. If you're doing that, let me know. I'll send my little brother Joe to your house. It is OK to invest while paying a house mortgage but you should try to accelerate your mortgage payments and get the house paid off ASAP. Once you get the house paid off, you'll funnel all those payments you aren't making anymore into investments.

- Insure your home if you own one and insure your personal possessions for full replacement coverage whether you own a house or not. Most renters skip this. Don't.

- If you have family members who depend on your income, buy term life insurance from a company that is highly rated for financial soundness. Check with organizations like Select Quote (1-800-343-1985). They will search for the least expensive policy and won't charge for the service. When you're determining how much life insurance you need, don't forget to factor in social security survivor's benefits. Contact social security and ask for a "Request For Earnings and Benefits Statement" which, when completed, will tell you roughly how much your survivors will receive if you die. Avoid whole life or universal life. Those two insurance products are a mix of life insurance and investments. Savvy people who understand those policies usually don't buy them; that's why they sell so many of them. Keep in mind that the cost of term life insurance goes up as you age, so plan to save enough so you can drop it by age 55 or so. If you have enough money to live on, you don't need life insurance.

- If you don't have disability insurance through your job, buy it. You're much more likely to become disabled than to die. Social Security Disability Insurance is very difficult to get so don't count on it to protect you. A good article on the subject is "What to Look for in Disability Income Policies" by Peter C. Katt, (November 1992, *American Association of Individual Investors Journal*). By the way, the *AAII Journal* is an excellent resource for in-depth information on a variety of tough personal finance issues. It deals with difficult issues and does it well. Check it out at your local library or contact AAII at 625 N. Michigan Avenue, Chicago, IL 60611, (800) 428-2244. If you subscribe, you can download most of the back issues on its website at www.aaii.com.

- Buy good health insurance. Avoid managed care (which usually means "less care"). All health care is managed now but some plans are more managed than others. Until politicians find the courage to fix the broken health-care system, health care will remain the biggest threat to financial freedom for average people. Individual states are initiating some reforms, so it is possible to buy health insurance in some states without underwriting, which is the process of weeding out people who might use the insurance.

- Get decent car insurance. Go with a $500 deductible on both collision (crashing while moving) and comprehensive (a tree falls on your car) and drop both of those if your car drops to $2000 or $3000 in value. If you use insurance to pay for small things under $500, you'll just force your premiums up, so it doesn't pay to go with smaller deductibles. Also keep in mind that if you have a collision there is a 50/50 chance the other guy will be at fault and pay the entire repair bill.

Many of you are reading this and feeling that you will never be able to do all of these things and you're thinking about giving up. That's how we felt a few years ago and if we can achieve our goals, so can you. Stick it out and forge ahead. You'll get there eventually. Just don't skip any important steps along the way.

HOMEWORK

Investing Knowledge . . .
Where to Get It

With the exception of IRS rules, there aren't too many things in personal finance that are very difficult to understand. The problem is, there are a whole bunch of easy things you need to grasp, and since they all interact, you've got to get your mind to hold a lot of things at once. It's getting your mind around all those things at one time, so you can see the whole picture, that's the difficult part. The only way to do it is to saturate your brain with information so your investment decisions become automatic, almost second nature. There's just no getting around it. You've got to read, and then read some more, and then read some more.

Unfortunately, there's a lot of bogus information out there and it can be difficult for beginners to separate the wheat from the chaff. We have read literally hundreds of books and thousands of articles about personal finance and we've kept track of our favorites. If you're just getting started we'd suggest that you spend about 5 hours per week learning the ropes and to make that easier for you, we've laid out a step-by-step self-education program that will fill your mind with some of the best information in the world of personal finance. We've carefully hand-picked every book, article, and website on the list. Our personal observations and comments follow some of the titles. Start by reading these 12 books and we suggest you read them in the order listed:

1. *Get a Financial Life: Personal Finance in Your Twenties and Thirties* by Beth Kobliner (Fireside, $12.00). A great book for beginners that covers a wide range of information from setting up bank accounts to selecting mutual funds.

2. *Personal Finance for Dummies* by Eric Tyson (IDG Books, $19.99). Tyson's book is fun to read, easy to understand, and one of the best books available on personal finance. A must read.

3. *How to Want What You Have: Discovering the Magic and Grandeur of Ordinary Existence* by Timothy Miller (Avon Books, $12.00). The title says it all. This book reveals important secrets about achieving happiness.

4. *The Handbook for No-Load Fund Investors* by Sheldon Jacobs (The No-Load Fund Investor, Inc., $45.00). This is the first financial how-to book we read. It consists primarily of mutual fund performance charts. Ignore them. Read the narrative section at the beginning of the book for an excellent primer on the mechanics of mutual funds.

5. *Simplify Your Life: 100 Ways to Slow Down and Enjoy the Things That Really Matter* by Elaine St. James (Hyperion, $9.95). One hundred creative, practical ideas that will improve the quality of your life. A real gem.

6. *Stocks for the Long Run: The Definitive Guide to Financial Market Returns and Long-Term Investment Strategies* by Jeremy J. Siegel (McGraw-Hill, $29.95). Dr. Siegel's book will calm your fears about investing in stocks over the long haul. This book about the history of the financial markets and what those historical returns might mean for you is fascinating.

7. *Taxes for Dummies* by Eric Tyson and David J. Silverman (IDS Books, $14.99). Eric Tyson again! Don't wait until tax time

to read this book. Read it cover to cover so you'll know how to incorporate tax issues into your day-to-day investment decisions.

8. *Living More with Less* by Doris Longacre (Herald Press, $12.99). This is a religion-based book written by a Mennonite woman. It provides suggestions about simple living based on the author's experiences and letters from others in the quest to simplify and improve their lives. The book may be hard to find but your library should be able to track it down.

9. *Common Sense on Mutual Funds: New Imperatives for the Intelligent Investor* by John Bogle (John Wiley & Sons, $24.95). John Bogle is the founder of the Vanguard Group of mutual funds. This guy knows as much about mutual funds as anyone, and he's not afraid to expose the dark spots. A must read.

10. *The Overworked American: The Unexpected Decline of Leisure* by Juliet B. Schor (Basic Books/Harper Collins, $14.00). Work consumes far too much of the average family's time. Why? This book will help you to understand the big picture and why it doesn't need to be this way.

11. *Stocks, Bonds, Bills, and Inflation: 1998 Yearbook* by Ibbotson Associates (Ibbotson Associates, $99.00 for the current version or $50.00 for a 2-year-old version). Spend several hours with this book to understand the historical returns of stocks, bonds, cash, and inflation. Examine individual years and decades. Look at historical worst-case scenarios and visualize yourself in their midst. What would you do? How would you feel? What would have happened if you panicked and sold your stock holdings (or held what you had and bought more) during some of history's worst declines? These types of psychological exercises will prepare you to face risks in the financial markets. You can find this book in most large libraries or buy one that's a couple years old for $50.

12. *Wall Street Words: An Essential A to Z Guide for Today's Investor* by David Logan Scott (Houghton Mifflin Co., $12.00). Buy

this book and keep it at your side while studying other resources for quick access to clear and concise definitions of investment words.

When you have completed the twelve books, move on to these magazine and Internet articles. You'll need to find back issues at your library or on the Internet at the addresses listed. We have added comments parenthetically after some titles.

"What to Look for in Disability Income Policies" by Peter C. Katt, *Association of American Individual Investors Journal*, November 1992.

"The Health Care Labyrinth" by Lawrence A. Armour, *Money Magazine*, September 1998.

"The Bear Look," *AAII Journal*, February 1997. (A history of bear markets)

"A Series of Gambles" by Jonathan Burton, *Dow Jones Asset Management Magazine*, Nov/Dec 1998. (The psychology of investing)

"Don't Believe the Bull: Bond Funds Do Have a Place" by Jason Zweig, *Money Magazine*, June 1998. (Superb article about bond mutual funds)

"Basic Truths About Asset Allocation: A Consensus View Among the Experts" by William Reichenstein, *AAII Journal*, October 1996.

"Make Your Money Work for You" by Jerry Edgerton, *Money Magazine* (Bonus Section), January 1997. (Unique and interesting perspectives on decisions every investor will face)

"The Big Bad News About Fee Only Financial Planners" by Ruth Simon, *Money Magazine*, December 1995.

"Peering Into a Fund's Past Can't Tell You All You Need to Know About Its Future" by Jason Zweig, *Money Magazine*, October 1996.

"The Age of Indexing" by Joseph Nocera, *Money Magazine*, April 1999.

"Roth IRA May Lack Protection From Creditors," James L. Dam, *Lawyers Weekly USA: The National Newspaper for Small Firm Lawyers*, February 9, 1998. (Find this article at www.lawyers weekly.com/featira2.htm. If you didn't know that some retirement plans are protected from creditors and want more information, this article includes references to relevant state laws.)

"Distributions Before 59 ½: How to Avoid the Penalty for Early Withdrawals" by Clark M. Blackman II and Kathleen A. Canty, *AAII Journal*, August 1995.

"Retirement Savings: Choosing a Withdrawal Rate That Is Sustainable" by Philip L. Cooley, et al., *AAII Journal*, February 1998.

"Three Keys to Shaping a Smarter Portfolio" by Lani Luciano, *Money Magazine* (Bonus Section), November 1997. (How long your money will last at various spending rates)

"The 5 Percent Solution" by Peter Lynch, *Worth Magazine*, April 1996, or find it on the web at www.worth.com/articles/Z9604E02.html

"Living on Retirement Savings in a World of Uncertain Return Patterns" by Maria Crawford Scott, *AAII Journal*, August 1996.

The following articles can be found at Vanguard's Internet site. The 8 in the first group are transcripts of speeches by John Bogle, founder of Vanguard, and they provide his insights into some important facets of mutual fund investing. These articles can be found at http://www.vanguard.com/educ/lib/bogle/ixbogle.html. The 11 articles in the Plain Talk Series are also found on Vanguard's website (http://www.vanguard.com/catalog/lit/catlistPT.html) and provide some of the most valuable educational information that we've seen to date. Don't miss them. Our comments are added parenthetically after some titles.

The Bogle Perspectives

1. The Clash of the Cultures in Investing: Complexity vs. Simplicity

2. Investing with Simplicity (Discussion about the costs of complex investment strategies)

3. The Death Rattle of Indexing (Index funds and investment myths)

4. The Four Dimensions of Investment Return (About risk, reward, cost, and time)

5. Happiness or Misery? Investment Performance in an Age of Investment Relativism

6. Bogle on Investment Performance and the Law of Gravity

7. Nothing Fails Like Success (Discussion of large mutual funds)

8. The Investment Outlook and Strategies in our Global World

Plain Talk Series

1. Plain Talk: Bond Fund Investing

2. Plain Talk: Taxes and Mutual Funds

3. Plain Talk: International Investing

4. Plain Talk: Perspectives on Market Volatility

5. Plain Talk: Realistic Expectations for Stock Market Returns

6. Plain Talk: Index Investing

7. Plain Talk: Mutual Fund Basics

8. Plain Talk: Mutual Fund Costs

9. Plain Talk: Dollar Cost Averaging

10. Plain Talk: Bear Markets

11. Plain Talk: Five Myths About Indexing

You'll also want to check out the following four Internet sites:

1. www.bondsonline.com (This is a great place to learn about bonds. Focus on the Treasuries and Corporates sections.)
2. www.investinginbonds.com (Another great site for learning about bonds.)
3. www.money.com/fundamentalist (Jason Zweig of *Money Magazine* is one of our favorite financial authors and some of his insightful articles can be found at this website.)
4. www.georgetown.edu/research/ihcrp/hipaa (Specific information, broken down by state about your rights to access health care.)

Once you learn the basics you'll want to keep up with financial industry changes, tax code changes, and new academic studies that can impact your investments. We subscribe to *Money Magazine* and it does a good job of keeping us up to date on evolving issues. We'd suggest that you choose a solid periodical like *Money, Kiplinger*, or some other well-established personal finance magazine, while also subscribing to the *American Association of Individual Investors Journal* for its scholarly, in-depth, and insightful analyses of the investment issues that we all face on a day-to-day basis. Addresses and information follow:

- American Association of Individual Investors, 625 N. Michigan Avenue, Chicago, IL 60611 (1-800-428-2244). Membership fee, which includes a subscription to the *AAII Journal*, is $49.00. For more information, visit its website at www.aaii.com. Members of AAII receive access to back issues of the *AAII Journal* through the website.
- *Money Magazine*, P.O. Box 60001, Tampa, FL 33660 (1-800-633-9970). A 1-year subscription runs about $29.95. *Money's*

web address is www.money.com and its E-mail address is subsvcs@money.customersvc.com.

Thousands of average families are doing a great job of managing their investments and there's no reason you can't do it, too. So brew a cup of tea, flip a CD into the stereo, and curl up in your favorite recliner with a stack of books and magazines at your side. Before you know it, you'll be investing like a pro. You'll be in good hands: your own.

Good luck and happy investing!

PART EIGHT

INVESTING

The investment world is like a carnival with so many bright lights, noises, seductions, and distractions that it's hard to stay focused on the dull, quiet, boring things that may mean the difference between success and failure. There are a million ways to mess up our investments and the best strategy is to shun all the flashy stuff and avoid mistakes. Investing isn't a game or a sport. It's a serious business that will help determine how we spend the time we have left on this earth. Investing matters. It's important enough to take the time to get it right.

STOCKS

Breaking Through the Minimum Wage Mentality

Try visualizing each dollar you've saved; all of them laid out on a table. All of a sudden, they come to life and start milling around, thousands of them. They've all got little feet and hands and heads. Their little leader comes up to you and announces that all these little dollars are ready to go to work, and anything they earn, they'll give to you. They will work for you so you don't have to. Just imagine all those little guys marching out the door to go to work every morning. They're dressed in coveralls, lace-up work boots, those $1.29 yellow chore gloves, and they're all carrying steel lunch buckets and thermos bottles. They're loyal, predictable, reliable, and humble. We understand them and we're comfortable with them. We like them. Unfortunately, they aren't paid very well; in fact, they are hardly paid anything at all. Although we like them, they're terrible earners and by the time we subtract inflation there isn't much extra left over for us. They are savings accounts and interest-bearing checking accounts, the unskilled, minimum wage workers of the financial world.

All of our dollars come to us as unskilled workers because we're paid cash for our labor. We spend most of it and put the rest in a savings or a checking account where it earns the equivalent of the minimum wage, or possibly even slave wages, because some checking accounts don't pay anything at all. Slavery is legal in the financial world. As we become more astute investors, we move up to CDs or bonds and our workers earn a little more than the minimum wage, but not much more. CDs are safe, reliable, and understandable, so many of us keep our little workers at this wage for a long time, always wearing coveralls, lace-up work boots, and yellow chore gloves. We keep our workers at these low wages because it feels so safe. And we love them.

Years pass. We're still toiling away at our jobs and our little workers are toiling at theirs. Our lives are unchanged and there's no end in sight, so we feel a twinge of resentment toward our low wage workers and toy with the idea of trading them in for little worker dollars who wear business suits, carry attaché cases, and talk on cellular phones. But deep down we don't like those characters. They're complicated, unreliable, pretentious little weasels that have been known to turn on their owners; even push them out windows in 1929. "But 1929 was a long time ago," we say to ourselves, "and most of the time these worker dollars earn far more than the minimum wage." Still, we don't trust them so we think about hiring an overseer, sometimes called a broker or a financial planner, to keep an eye on these rascals so they don't turn on us. But we read or hear that overseers can't always be relied on to protect us. Sometimes they turn on us, too. So what can we do?

Wouldn't it be nice if we didn't need stocks in our portfolios? If we could just get a guaranteed return at a high rate, life would be so much easier and much more secure. Unfortunately, stocks are needed because they return more over time than other investments and we're not likely to achieve financial freedom without them. Stocks have returned about 10 percent per year on average since 1926 while bonds and cash have returned about 5 percent and 4 percent respectively.* Reduce those returns by 3 percent for inflation and you have a real return of about 7 percent for stocks and only 1 percent to 2 percent for bonds and cash, so families just can't afford to pass up stocks. We'd like to because they scare us, but we can't. So if we're stuck with them, it will pay to understand them.

Investing in Stocks Is Not a Zero Sum Game

As children, my siblings and I would occasionally set up a lemonade stand and sell Kool-Aid (never lemonade for some strange reason) at a nickel a glass. We'd borrow a few bucks from our parents, buy paper cups, sugar, and drink powder, and open our store on a card table. At supper time we'd close it up and split the take after offering to pay our parents back and gladly accepting their refusal. If you can understand lemonade stands, you know most of what you need to know about stocks.

The main difference is that most businesses, unlike our lemonade stand, don't have benevolent parents to provide start-up capital, so they either borrow what they need and promise to pay back their lenders at a fixed rate, or they issue stock and let their stockholders share in ownership of the company. If the drink powder, cups, and sugar for our lemonade stand had been purchased with money raised by issuing stock, at the end of the day we'd have either rolled the profits into the business and opened a second stand the next day, in hopes of doubling our profit, or perhaps we'd have stayed with one stand and split any profits among all the stockholders in proportion to the amount of stock owned. Profits distributed in that way are called *dividends*. The value of each share in our lemonade

---

*E. Tyson, *Personal Finance for Dummies* (Foster City, CA: IDG Books Worldwide, Inc., 1996, p. 201).

stand would go up and down on a daily basis per the perceived value of our stand's current and future profits, so if we sell our share of the stand for less than we paid, we create a capital loss. Sell it for more and we create a *capital gain.*

Large, well-established companies usually don't grow as fast as small companies so they tend to distribute their profits to shareholders in the form of dividends, which are taxed as ordinary income. Since they're large, well-established, and have a steady stream of dividends, their share prices tend to fluctuate less. Small companies tend to roll more of their profits back into the business for expansion. Their share prices tend to be more volatile. Although the upside potential is greater, so is the downside. Dividends are often minimal but capital gains, which are taxed at special, often lower rates, can be significant in small companies.

Investing in stocks is *not* a zero sum game. All investors can make money in stocks at the same time; there doesn't have to be a loser for every winner. Kids on another block can open a lemonade stand and make money, too. Investing in stocks is simply investing in businesses and sharing in their fortunes, whether good or bad, that's all. It's not gambling if done correctly.

Stocks Are Best for the Long Run

Dr. Jeremy Siegel, in his book, *Stocks for the Long Run: The Definitive Guide to Financial Market Returns and Long-Term Investment Strategies,* provides one of the most valuable pieces of information we've seen in the following chart. Understanding his chart is much of what you'll need to know about investing in stocks, so take a moment to study it.

After subtracting the rate of inflation from the returns of stocks, bonds, and cash, Dr. Siegel determined that the worst-case scenario for stocks since 1802 has been better than the worst-case scenario for either bonds or cash for holding periods of 10 years or more. So,

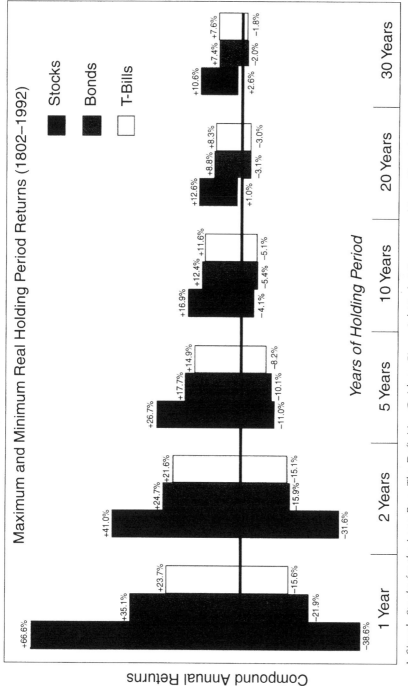

Long-Term Investing

Maximum and Minimum Real Holding Period Returns (1802–1992)

Stocks
Bonds
T-Bills

Compound Annual Returns

Years of Holding Period

1 Year
+66.6%
+35.1%
+23.7%
−15.6%
−21.9%
−38.6%

2 Years
+41.0%
+24.7% +21.6%
−15.9% −15.1%
−31.6%

5 Years
+26.7%
+17.7% +14.9%
−11.0% −10.1% −8.2%

10 Years
+16.9%
+12.4% +11.6%
−4.1% −5.4% −5.1%

20 Years
+12.6%
+8.8% +8.3%
+1.0%
−3.1% −3.0%

30 Years
+10.6%
+7.4% +7.6%
+2.6%
−2.0% −1.8%

J. Siegel, *Stocks for the Long Run: The Definitive Guide to Financial Market Returns and Long-Term Investment Strategies,* McGraw-Hill, 1998, p. 27. Reproduced with permission.

while stocks are far more volatile than bonds or cash over short periods, the longer you hold them the less risk you incur. Since 1802, stocks have never produced a negative inflation adjusted return if held for 20 years or more. Although stocks are quite risky if held for only a year or two, over long periods, the safest investment has been stocks, not bonds or cash. What does that mean for us? Invest in stocks, but only if we can hold them for 5 years or more.

Stocks can hurt us if we aren't investing for the long run or if we don't diversify, which we'll discuss later, but fear of stocks is way overblown. We need them because of their superior returns and if we can hold them long enough, their volatility relative to bonds and cash virtually disappears. So if we diversify and hold our stocks for a long time, we can put them to work right beside our low wage workers. We need them both; bonds and cash for shorter term needs and to prevent our entire portfolio from tanking if there's a stock market meltdown, and stocks for better returns over the long haul.

Our dollars replace us in the workforce. Some of them are low or minimum wage workers who will wear coveralls and yellow chore gloves, and we love those workers because they are safe. But some of our workers must wear business suits and carry attaché cases and cellular phones. Although we may never feel entirely comfortable with them, we need them for their earning power. So break out of the minimum wage mentality and give them a chance, or more importantly, give them plenty of time. Given time, workers in business suits who carry attaché cases and talk on cellular phones aren't so bad after all.

BONDS

Smoothing Out the Dips

Pretend that your life savings are on the line and you're in a market like 1973–1974 when stocks lost 48 percent, almost half their value. How would you react? Would you have the courage to hold your ground or would you panic and sell your holdings at terrible prices? According to the Vanguard Financial Group, an investor who had $10,000 invested in stocks during that period lost about $4800 while a portfolio composed of 60 percent stocks and 40 percent bonds lost only $2900.* Twenty-nine percent versus forty-eight percent; that is the power of bonds.

Most of the money is made in stocks, but they're a rough ride. Sure, big companies have returned about 11 percent on average over the last 70 years, but in 1931 they lost 43 percent while gaining 54 percent in 1933. Since you never know when something like that will hit, it isn't wise to put all your money into stocks. That's where bonds come in. They smooth the ride and get you through the rough times. And when you're relying on your stash to pay the bills, bonds provide a steady and reliable stream of income.

---

*"Plain Talk—Bear Markets," Vanguard Financial Group, 1999; www.vanguard
.com/catalog/lit/catlistPT.html.

Because stocks can be extremely volatile over short periods, it is important to plan for those occasional precipitous declines with the idea of preventing the need to sell our stocks at low prices. It is easy to know the daily value of our stock holdings and we tend to form a mental picture of money when we think about them, but what we really own are buildings, factory machinery, inventory, and such. When the stock market collapses, we still own those businesses. The buildings are still standing, the machinery is still humming away, and the inventory is still in the warehouse. So why is it that investors tend to be happy to hold on to those businesses yesterday when they could have been sold for $1000, yet are quick to get rid of them today for $500? Let's phrase the question another way. If you own a business that you believe to be worth $1000, what would you rather have, the business or $500? The business, of course! So it makes no sense to sell your businesses when the market tanks, does it? But that's what many people do. Will you sell when the market falls? Or will you be able to wait it out? That will probably depend on whether you have bonds in your portfolio to calm your nerves and cover your expenses. Bonds make it possible to gut it out.

Bonds aren't businesses, they're loans you make to government entities or corporations at a fixed rate. These loans provide regular dividends and the principal is returned to you when the term of the loan expires. They're a lot like CDs, really, the main difference being that they're actively traded among investors, a process that works like this:

- You've got $10,000 sitting in the bank earning 2 percent interest and you realize that it's not too bright for you to settle for a measly 2 percent.

- You call your friendly discount broker and he tells you that some poor sucker loaned $10,000 to the Rush Limbaugh Women's Clothing Company at 6 percent and he wants to sell that bond. "OK," you tell your broker, "I'll get back to you."

- You can't imagine that any woman would want to wear clothing with Rush Limbaugh's mug on the tag, so you're skeptical and ask yourself, "Do I really want to loan money to this company?"

- So you check with one of the rating companies such as Moody's and learn to your surprise that Rush's company is doing well. His debt is rated "Aaa" by Moody's, which is the best rating possible, and means there is the smallest degree of default risk (check at www.moodys.com for ratings definitions). Of course, lower rated bonds would demand higher rates to compensate investors for the extra risk, but that's not a problem here.

- But there is another problem. Interest rates have gone up since the guy who wants to sell his Rush Limbaugh bond bought it at 6 percent. Today you can loan your money to Aaa-rated corporations and get 7 percent. There's no way you're going to assume this guy's 6 percent loan when you could earn 7 percent somewhere else. So he's got to cut his price enough to make up for the difference between the 6 percent you'll get when you buy his loan and the 7 percent rate you could get somewhere else. How much will he have to cut his price? Well, it depends on the duration of the loan. If he's loaned the money to Rush for 30 years, he'll have to cut it a whole lot more than if the loan is for 5 years to make up for all those years of inferior dividends. And it's not purely a matter of interest rates either. I might be more reluctant to loan money for 30 years than for 5. It depends on my perception of the company's future. But the important thing to remember is that bond prices go down when interest rates go up and vice-versa, and the prices of long-term bonds go up and down much more than the prices of short-term bonds when interest rates change.

- So, you decide to buy the Rush Limbaugh bond. You pay $9000 for the $10,000 bond. You continue to earn 6 percent per year on $10,000 and when the term of the loan ends, Rush will return $10,000 to you. But since you only paid $9000, you'll actually be earning the equivalent of 7 percent on the $9000 you paid for the bond. That's how bonds work. When you buy a bond, you're simply loaning your money to a government entity or to a business at the going rate, or, you're buying a loan that someone made in the past at a price that will compensate you for any increase in rates since the loan originated, or at a price that compensates the seller for any decrease in rates since the original loan was made.

Loans to corporations aren't federally insured so their rates are usually a tad higher than government bonds depending on the quality of the debt. But you can loan money to the government, too. Loans to the U.S. Treasury are the safest loans in existence because they're backed by the full faith and credit of the U.S. government, plus they're free of state and local taxes. But their prices go up and down just like corporate bonds so if you're forced to sell when interest rates are up, you could lose money. You can also loan your money to municipalities. Municipal bonds aren't federally insured but the dividends they pay aren't taxed on the federal level, and sometimes they aren't taxed on the state or local level either. So why buy Treasury or corporate bonds? Because municipal bond rates are lower and it doesn't pay to buy them unless your federal tax bracket is 28 percent or higher.

Bank CDs can be like bonds, too. They're federally insured and can be purchased through brokers. If you decide to cash in one of these brokered CDs before it matures, you'll need to find a buyer and you may get more or less than your original investment, depending on prevailing rates when you sell.

One nice thing about individual bonds is that you always have the option to hold them until they mature. Barring default, which isn't likely if you stick to highly rated issues, you're assured of a steady stream of dividends and the return of your principal at maturity. But you can also invest in bonds through mutual funds. In a bond mutual fund your money is pooled with the money of other investors and bonds are purchased on the group's behalf. Shares in bond mutual funds don't mature like individual bonds. Nevertheless, low-cost bond mutual funds offer other advantages like diversification and simplicity. We prefer low-cost bond mutual funds for those reasons. But do keep in mind that bond prices, while not as volatile as stocks, do have their own bear markets with price declines of 15 percent or more in a year. For details, read Vanguard's "Plain Talk: Bear Markets" at www.vanguard.com/catalog/lit/catlistPT.html.

If you want a guaranteed return that's adjusted for inflation, buy Treasury Inflation-Indexed Securities. Although we think we'll do better in the long run with our bond mutual fund, there's no better guarantee than the one offered through Treasury Inflation-Indexed Securities. To learn more about them, and for tons of information about bonds in general, check out www.bondsonline.com and www.investinginbonds.com. Whether you choose municipal bonds, corporate bonds, treasuries, or brokered CDs, bonds are an integral part of any carefully constructed portfolio.

CASH

A Risky Investment

My grandfather was a young man with a family when the stock market crashed in 1929. After the smoke cleared, sometime in the 1940s, he bought some stock that was supposed to be solid, but went belly up. So, his sons and daughters learned as children that stocks were like gambling with the odds stacked against them; worth nothing more than the paper they were printed on. My father, understandably, has shied away from stocks and the fears of my father and grandfather have trickled down to me. I had no intention of touching stocks with a 10-foot pole until a threat to my livelihood sent me scurrying to the bookstore to learn how to achieve economic security, so my family's financial survival wouldn't be tied to the whims of politicians or business executives. I studied . . . and studied . . . and studied. It is no exaggeration to say that I read literally hundreds of books and magazine articles about investing and the history of financial assets. I flooded my brain with the findings of the best minds in the world of personal finance, and it was through that baptism of facts that my psyche was purged of the irrational fears and misconceptions spawned by the stock market crash of 1929. The two most fundamental misconceptions that still plague many investors are these:

1. Most investors believe that stocks pose far more risk than they do, but consider these facts from *Stocks for the Long Run* by Dr. Jeremy Siegel:

   - ". . . [M]oney put in stocks at the August 1929 market peak accumulated to a greater sum over 30 years than money put into bonds over the same period.

   - Even the worst 30-year post-1926 returns for stocks, which occurred from 1960–1990, is almost three times the best 30-year returns for bonds and bills.

   - You can mix and match any 30-year period in stocks to any in bonds and bills and find it impossible not to find stocks coming out on top.

   - Even with holding periods as short as five years, stocks out-perform long and short term bonds by a four-to-one margin since 1926. . . ."*

2. Most individual investors view cash as a safe haven, especially cash that is federally insured such as U.S. Treasury Bills or short-term CDs. As shown previously in the chart on page 161, Dr. Siegel compares the returns of stocks, bonds, and cash (represented by Treasury Bills) with inflation factored into those returns (referred to as "real return"). The chart reveals that the worst real return for stocks over any 10-, 20-, or 30-year period since 1802 is better than the worst real returns for bonds or cash over those same time periods! So in a very real sense, cash, when held 10 years or more, has been riskier than stocks in terms of worst-case scenarios.

I've eliminated most of my irrational fears and misconceptions about the financial markets, yet I hold out less hope for finding iron-clad security than my grandfather. He feared stocks but found solace in cash; I fear both and find solace in neither. What I do have,

---

*J. Siegel, *Stocks for the Long Run: The Definitive Guide to Financial Market Returns and Long Term Investment Strategies* (New York: McGraw-Hill Publishing, 1994, p. 29).

though, is a good understanding of the risks I face, and very good odds of outliving my assets by owning a well-balanced portfolio that eliminates as much risk as possible. But there is no complete security in the financial markets; all of my holdings are subject to decline, including my cash, which is vulnerable to the erosion of inflation and taxes. Cash is likely to produce no return or even a negative return after taxes and inflation if held for long periods of time.

So, why have any cash? We hold approximately 10 percent to 15 percent cash in our portfolio plus an emergency cash reserve. If stock and bond prices both plunge at the same time, we'll plan to use cash to cover some of our expenses while we hunker down and ride it out. If stock prices plunge terribly low, we might use cash to buy more at bargain prices. Having cash makes it less likely that we'll panic or sell when prices are low. Cash will buy us time and so far, time has healed most wounds in the financial markets.

Whether consciously or not, we're all on the path to financial security and eventually most of us will have it, even if it means eking out a survival on social security. But for those of us who aren't paid big salaries and want out early, there is no investment in existence that is insulated from the ravages of inflation, taxes, and market swings, while also providing enough growth and income to cover our expenses and set us free before we're old. Each asset class (stocks, bonds, or cash) will do some of those things, but none will do it all. There is no comfort in this business of investing, no safe haven. Our only hope is to acquire the right mix of stocks, bonds, and cash and fine tune the weighting of each so that together, the entire portfolio will be shielded from the ravages of inflation, taxes, market swings, and other risks. No asset class within the portfolio is shielded from all those things, but the portfolio as a whole, if we construct it carefully, will have the highest probability of holding together to meet our needs and set us free.

ALLOCATION

Asset Allocation—The Family's Most Important Investment Decision

I created a great chili recipe. It's called Bill's Chili and it is the best chili in the world, bar none. I've got a friend from high school who makes good chili, too. He thinks his is better but he knows, deep down in his heart, that mine's the best. My chili has three ingredients: beans, meat, and sauce. When I serve it, people say, "Bill, this is the best chili I've ever had." They don't say, "I like this meat and sauce and beans." They say they like the chili. If instead of chili, I served a bowl of beans, a bowl of sauce, and a plate of ground beef, it wouldn't be the same, would it? Same ingredients, yes, but a mouthful of beans, then sauce, and then beef does not equal three mouthfuls of chili. It isn't the beef or the sauce or the beans that makes chili what it is; it's putting them all together and getting just the right amount of beef and just the right amount of sauce and just the right amount of beans. It's about getting the mix right.

Investing is like chili. It's about getting just the right amount of stocks, just the right amount of bonds, and just the right amount of cash. The term for this is *asset allocation,* and how you allocate your holdings is the most important investment decision you'll make. In fact, most experts agree that asset allocation has far more to do with how your portfolio will do over time than all other factors combined. Few investors believe this, though. Many agonize over things like picking the right mutual fund or timing their purchases. But those decisions pale in comparison to the impact that asset allocation is likely to have on a portfolio over time. So, when it comes to investing, avoiding mistakes when deciding how to divvy up your holdings is crucial.

The first step in getting your allocation right is to develop the right mindset. Stop compartmentalizing. In other words, banish thoughts like these:

- What should I do with this account?
- I'll make account number 1 really safe but since account number 2 is "found money," I'll gamble with it.
- I can afford to lose this account, but not this one.
- I'm comfortable with the way this account is performing so I don't want to mess with it. I'll just focus on these accounts over here.

Apply allocation decisions to your entire portfolio, not to pieces of it. It's like chili; you can't change the beans without changing the chili, and it's the chili that matters, not the beans.

Let's say you owe $22,000 on your house and you're carrying about $2000 in credit card debt. You have two $20,000 CDs, $1900 in your checking account, about $8000 worth of household goods, $9000 in a savings account IRA at a local bank, $4000 in a credit union savings account, 2 cars worth roughly $12,000 total, $3000 in a passbook savings account, and $31,000 in bonds in a 401(k). None of this was planned, it just happened, and you have no idea what to do with all of it.

First deal with the house. Although you can include it as an asset on a net worth statement, it can't be converted to cash if you need it, so it's not an investment. Same goes for cars and personal possessions. Besides, when it comes right down to it, most personal possessions like lawn mowers, TVs, or clothing, are actually liabilities because they need to be replaced when they wear out and some of them need to be maintained at considerable cost of time and money. Financially, we'd probably be better off without them. So exclude cars, house, and personal possessions and make a list of what's left:

- $20,000 CD—matures in 3 months
- $20,000 CD—matures in 6 months
- $1900—checking account
- $3000—passbook savings account
- $9000—IRA in bank savings account
- $31,000—401(k) (invested in a bond fund)
- $4000—credit union savings account

  $88,900—Total

Take $2000 out of the credit union savings account and pay off (and then cut up) the credit card. Carrying credit card debt when you have money in the bank is just plain dumb.

Assuming you have all the insurance coverage you need, set aside enough cash to cover 6 months to 1 year of living expenses. For us, roughly $25,000 is about right, so the $20,000 CD that matures in 3 months, the $1900 checking account, and the $3000 passbook savings account will be set aside as an emergency cash reserve. Keep about $2000 in a dividend-paying credit union checking account and put the rest in a good-performing, low-expense money market mutual fund. If you don't include your emergency stash in the investment allocation, and you shouldn't, you're left with this:

- $20,000 CD—matures in 6 months
- $9000—IRA in bank savings account

- $31,000—401(k) (invested in a bond fund)
- $2000—credit union savings account

  $64,000—Total

Next, we'd probably pay off the $22,000 we owe on the house. Of course, many would argue that it makes sense to continue carrying a mortgage as long as one can reasonably expect to make more in the financial markets than the rate of the mortgage (minus the tax deduction). But that's often a hairsplitting decision requiring a computer and a crystal ball, so we'd pay off the mortgage unless we could invest the money at a guaranteed rate that exceeds the after-tax mortgage rate. In this scenario, we'd take the $20,000 CD that matures in 6 months and apply it to the house when it matures. We might even pay it off before it matures, but that would depend on the mortgage rate, the CD rate, and any applicable early withdrawal penalty. We'd also take the $2000 remaining in the credit union savings account and apply it to the house and close the savings account. Now you're down to this:

- $9000—IRA in bank savings account
- $31,000—401(k) (invested in a bond fund)

  $40,000—Total

Next, grab a calculator and determine the current allocation. There's a total of $40,000 with $31,000 in bonds and $9000 in cash. You're asking yourself these two questions:

1. $9000 in cash is _____ percent of the $40,000 total?
2. $31,000 in bonds is _____ percent of the $40,000 total?

To get the answers, hit these keys on the calculator: 9000 ÷ 40,000% and 31,000 ÷ 40,000%. The answer is 22.5 percent in cash and 77.5 percent in bonds. That is a terrible allocation and it needs to be fixed.

There are a couple of ways to determine the right allocation. The best way is to utilize mean-variance optimization, which is a complex mathematical process to determine an asset mix that will provide the least amount of risk for a given return. Essentially you ask, "If I want my portfolio to produce 9 percent (or whatever return you choose), what mix is likely to produce the 9 percent I want with the least amount of risk?" Most institutional investors (pension funds, endowment funds, etc.) use some form of this computer-generated process. We'd suggest that you check out a new Internet site called Financial Engines at www.financialengines.com. For $14.95 you get access to some incredibly sophisticated asset allocation advice based on the work of Nobel Laureate, William Sharpe. Also review the October 1996 issue of the *American Association of Individual Investors*. William Reichenstein examined the allocation recommendations of some prominent financial firms and eminent experts and he found that they were all recommending similar allocations for typical investors. Of course, not all of us are "typical" investors and there are reasons to stray from the norm, but for most of us, there is a mix in these recommendations that is probably about right:

Asset Allocation for the "Typical" Investor: The Broad Consensus

	Stocks (%)	Bonds (%)	Cash (%)
High-risk investors; young investors	70–80	15–25	0–5
Medium-risk investors; investors approaching retirement	60	30–40	0–10
Low-risk investors; retiring investors and retirees	40–50	40–50	10–20
Investors over age 70	20–30	60	10–20

From W. Reichenstein, "Basic Truths About Asset Allocation: A Consensus View Among the Experts," *American Association of Individual Investors Journal,* October 1996. Reproduced with permission.

It's a good idea to include a good portion of international holdings, probably about 20–30 percent of your total stock allocation. So for every $1000 you have in stocks, consider investing $200–300 in overseas companies with the remaining $700–800 in a broad mix of large, medium, and small companies domiciled in the United States. It is widely believed that international stocks will likely increase the long-term return of a portfolio while actually decreasing its volatility.

Let's say you're a typical low-risk investor nearing retirement. You decide to go with 40 percent in stocks, 50 percent in bonds, and 10 percent in cash, which is consistent with the recommendations in the foregoing figure. So if you have $40,000 to invest as in our previous example, here's how you'd split it up:

Stocks: $16,000 (40% of $40,000)
          international stocks: $4800 (30% of $16,000)
          United States stocks: $11,200 (70% of $16,000)

Bonds: $20,000 (50% of $40,000)

Cash: $4000 (10% of $40,000)

Deciding how to divvy up your portfolio between stocks, bonds, and cash is the most important investment decision you'll make, and it comprises much of what you need to know about investing. So, find a comfort zone on the previous figure and start moving toward an allocation that's right for you. It's all about getting a decent return with a level of risk that won't keep you awake at night.

FUNDS

No-Load Mutual Funds—
The Way Families Should Invest

What's better, buying individual securities or investing in stocks, bonds, and cash through mutual funds? We prefer funds. In fact, we like them so much that all of our investments are in them. Here's why:

- When you invest in a mutual fund, you're pooling your money with money belonging to other investors. It's like getting together with your neighbors over coffee and saying, "None of us has the time or the expertise to choose individual securities, so let's all put our cash together and hand it over to a firm of money managers. We'll let them invest it for us and give them a small percentage of the assets in the fund to pay for their services. If we all go in together, there will be enough money in the fund to invest in the stocks or bonds of a whole bunch of companies. If one or two fail, it won't ruin any of us because we'll be well diversified. Each year we'll divide up the profits (or losses) according to the number of shares each person has invested in the fund. We'll set it up so that anyone can get their money out at any time. When they do, they'll get whatever their share of the fund is worth at the end of the day they cash in."

- There are thousands of mutual funds, each investing in some segment of the financial markets. There are funds that invest in stocks, bonds, cash, gold, real estate, or some mix of the aforementioned. Some mutual funds are quite focused and invest only in small company stocks, short-term government bonds, health-care stocks, or some other narrow niche of the markets. There are mutual funds to meet almost every need.

- Mutual funds typically hold millions, even billions of dollars, so when they buy and sell, they can do so in bulk and pay reduced transaction costs. A small investor who moves a few thousand dollars at a time pays higher transaction costs.

- Funds are liquid. If you want out, just call them and they'll send you a check for the value of the shares you sell. Funds that invest in money markets (cash) often provide checks that can be written for amounts of approximately $250 or more.

- Adjusting your asset allocation is easy with mutual funds. If stock prices shoot up and you find that you're holding more stocks than you want, simply adjust your holdings with a toll-free call:

"Good afternoon, this is XYZ Investments. How can I help you?"
"I'd like to take $1000 out of my stock fund and switch it over to my bond fund."
"Sure! Just give me a few seconds . . . OK, that's done. Anything else I can help you with today?"

- Mutual funds are an inexpensive way to invest if you do it right. First, make sure that you don't pay sales commissions. Plenty of mutual funds are sold directly to the public without sales commissions, so it doesn't make sense to pay a hefty fee to get into a fund. Second, invest in a mutual fund that has low annual expenses. Annual expenses are listed in the fund's prospectus or on the fund's website. Look for the annual expense ratio. That's the percentage of your assets you'll pay each year to cover the fund's costs of managing your money, providing staff to take your calls, printing and mailing statements, and other expenses. We pay between two-tenths of 1 percent and six-tenths of 1 percent per year, much less than the average fund's cost of about 1.25 percent.

- Investing in a mutual fund is easy. If you know your name, address, phone and social security numbers, and who you want to list as beneficiary, you can fill out one of these applications. Simply fill out the application, put it in a postage-paid envelope with a check in the amount you want to invest, drop it in the mail, and you're done.

With kids, jobs, and everything else that life throws at us, who has time to research, purchase, and follow individual stocks and bonds? We sure don't. If you're like us, mutual funds are the way to go.

CHOOSING

Drowning in a Sea of Choices

We give up! Trying to pick mutual funds that will beat the market is a waste of time. It has involved hours and hours of pouring over the past returns of thousands of funds in an effort to find the next Peter Lynch or Warren Buffett. Sometimes we've guessed right and sometimes we haven't; but we'd have more money in our pockets today if we had just put all of our investments into index funds from day one.

Indexes such as the Standard & Poor's (S&P) 500 and the Dow Jones Industrial Average were created many years ago to track the progress of the stock market. It's a kind of shorthand, or benchmark; a single number that enables investors to know in a flash whether the market as a whole is up or down. Before indexes, all investors had were the individual prices of hundreds of companies, some up and some down. That was great if all you wanted to know was how your stocks were doing. But what if you wanted to know how the market was doing generally, or how one segment of the market was doing relative to another, or how your stocks were far-ing relative to the market as a whole? Therefore indexes like the Dow and the S&P 500 were created to provide benchmarks. Although the Dow and the S&P 500 are widely known, there are indexes that track the progress of countless segments of the financial markets; European stocks, short-term bonds, intermediate-term bonds, emerging market stocks, the total U.S. stock market, the total U.S. bond market, and many more. Indexes were simply measuring tools until 1976. That's when the first index mutual fund was created by John Bogle, founder of the Vanguard Group of Mutual Funds. In 1976, Mr. Bogle made it possible for individual investors to invest directly in a mutual fund that held the securities that made up the S&P 500. Since then many more index funds have been created.

But why would you want to buy the securities that make up an index? Common sense tells us that it is better to put our money into mutual funds run by expert stock and bond pickers who will buy good securities and avoid bad ones. The truth is, most professional money managers fail to beat the market averages over long periods and the ones that do are probably just lucky. Beating the averages is tough for most mutual funds to do consistently because investment styles go in and out of favor, trading and management expenses are higher in managed funds, and there is usually a huge inflow of cash coming into funds that are touted as last year's stars.

We've concluded that trying to pick mutual funds that will beat the market is a fool's game and we've been fools for playing it. So we put most of our money into *index funds.* The only exceptions are cash reserves, which aren't sold as index funds, and international funds, which appear to benefit from active management. So with the exception of our international and cash holdings, the funds we buy don't hire professional stock and bond pickers. They contain whatever securities are in the index they are trying to match and hold those securities through thick and thin. We invest almost exclusively in these funds: Vanguard Total Stock Market Index Fund (U.S. stocks), Vanguard International Growth Fund (international stocks), Vanguard Total Bond Market Index Fund (bonds),

Vanguard Short-Term Bond Index Fund (bonds), and Vanguard Prime Money Market Fund (cash).

By investing primarily in index funds, our investment expenses are minuscule with no sales commissions and low annual expenses. We receive top-notch customer service, virtual assurance that our index fund investments will perform in tandem with the market as a whole (before expenses), and simplicity. Plus, index funds, with the possible exception of international funds, are likely to produce a better return than most actively managed funds over long periods of time. Therefore, we believe they're the best choice for most individual investors with a few caveats:

- Although Vanguard has the lowest costs in the business, they also have a very confusing array of small fees aimed at traders and investors with small account balances. If you tend to move in and out of funds (which you shouldn't be doing), some of Vanguard's funds will make you pay for the privilege, so make sure you examine the rules before you buy. If you're just getting started and don't have much to invest, look for extra fees for accounts with low balances, portfolio fees, and account maintenance fees. Vanguard usually waives these $10 fees if you invest $10,000 or more in a fund or if you have $50,000 or more in total at Vanguard, so we don't pay them. Ten dollars doesn't sound like much, but if you have $600 in your account and you're zinged with fees totaling $20, that's the equivalent of annual expenses exceeding 3 percent! Invest your money elsewhere until you can scrape up enough to avoid those fees, or choose other Vanguard funds that don't charge them.

- Vanguard is a great company but they have a virtual lock on low-cost funds. If you want lots of fund choices with rock bottom expenses and a large, well-established fund family, Vanguard is the only game in town. That makes us uneasy. So far we've seen no evidence of the complacency, rigidity, and arrogance that tends to permeate monopolies, but we'll be keeping our eyes open.

- Although we prefer the simplicity of the Total Bond Market Index Fund for the majority of our bond investments, some might prefer individual corporate bonds, U.S. Treasury Bonds, or even CDs for the bond portion of their portfolio (and keep in mind that while CDs and treasuries are federally insured, corporates aren't). If you'd prefer this type of control over the total return you receive, all you need is a brokerage account, which you can open at most large mutual fund companies. If you decide to go that route, consider laddering your individual corporates, treasuries, and/or CDs. If you have $50,000, buy five $10,000 bonds that mature in 1, 2, 3, 4, and 5 years. When your first bond matures after one year, replace it with another that will mature in five years. When the second bond matures at the end of year number two, use the proceeds to purchase another that will mature in five. Repeat the process each year and you'll minimize the risk of being forced to reinvest everything at once when rates are terrible. Plus, you're never more than one year away from 20 percent of your bond holdings, which minimizes the chance you'll need to sell when bond prices are down.

- If you're in a 28 percent or higher tax bracket, consider tax-free municipal bonds. They're free from federal, and in some cases, state taxes. You can buy individual municipal bonds through a broker, which gives you the option of locking in a return if you hold until maturity, or for simplicity, choose a mutual fund like the USAA Tax-Exempt Intermediate-Term Fund (1-800-531-8448 or www.usaa.com) or the Vanguard Intermediate-Term Tax-Exempt Fund (1-800-871-3879 or www.vanguard.com). Municipal bonds aren't federally insured, so be sure to check their quality before buying individual bonds.

- You might also want to consider Treasury Inflation-Indexed Securities for the bond portion of your portfolio. They're backed by the full faith and credit of the U.S. government, they're free of state and local taxes, and they provide a guaranteed return that's adjusted annually for inflation. These securities are as close to a sure thing as you can get. Read more about them at www.bondsonline.com. Buy them through a broker on the secondary market or directly from the U.S. Treasury through "Treasury Direct" (1-800-943-6864 or www.publicdebt.treas.gov/sec/sectrdir.htm). If you use a broker, you'll pay a commission, but you'll know the rate of return before you buy. "Treasury Direct" is free, but you get a rate determined at auction. There's no way of knowing for sure what the rate will be, but you can check financial publications like Barron's for estimates.

We think low-cost index funds are the best way to invest in U.S. stocks and bonds. Of course, if you do that, it's likely your friends, coworkers, and family may tell you that their investments beat the pants off yours. Magazine articles will tout all of the year's top funds, and your index funds probably won't be there. You might even regret your decision in the short term, but if you stick it out for many years, with index funds you will probably achieve the highest returns possible without relying on luck. And unless you own a reliable crystal ball, in investing that's about as good as it gets.

WHEN

When to Buy, When to Sell, When to Adjust

Years ago we watched an old black-and-white TV show; it may have been Alfred Hitchcock, we're not sure, but we remember the story. It was about a mousy, balding, bespectacled civil servant who received a mysterious unsigned letter delivered to his desk. The letter said something like this: "I have developed a system that determines with 100 percent accuracy what the stock market will do. I am fabulously wealthy and have no need for more money but I want to help others become as rich as I am. I have selected you at random to benefit from my knowledge. Over the next several days you will receive letters that will prove to you that this is real. Tell no one else about this! Tomorrow the stock market will go up."

Our little man was a curious fellow and at the end of the day he verified that the prediction made in this odd letter had indeed been correct. The next day he received another note predicting that the stock market would go down, and sure enough, the market dropped that day. Several days and letters later, our little clerk was in a lather, desperately trying to find the source of these letters. Finally a letter arrived, with another correct prediction, and directions to mail his life's savings to a post office box, which of course, he did. A few days later our pathetic little man noticed a letter addressed to a coworker, crumpled up and tossed in the trash. He pulled it out, unfolded it, and was horrified to discover that it was the very same stock market letter he had received a few days ago, except for one thing. The stock market prediction in the coworker's letter was wrong.

A scam artist had sent out a whole bunch of letters on the first day. Half predicted the market would go up and half that it would go down. On the second day he sent another batch, but only to those who had received the correct prediction on the previous day. Again, one half predicted an up market and the other half predicted a down market. In the end the civil servant was the only one remaining. All predictions sent to him had been correct, by chance. Purely by chance.

Timing the market is enticing, isn't it? If you could take your money out of the stock market in time to avoid big declines, it would have a huge impact on your return. If you could put your money back into the market just before it started to take off again, well, the sky's the limit. Your family would be wealthy in short order. Market timing is a wonderful concept. Unfortunately, it doesn't work. Don't buy newsletters that promise to get you in and out at the right times and don't try to do it yourself. Here's why:

- To time the market, *you must be right twice.* You need to know when to get out, but it's just as important to know when to get back in, and nobody has been able to do that consistently. Chances are you won't be able to do it either.

- One of the reasons market timing fails is that the market generally produces its gains very quickly. In the 1980s, 10 days accounted for 40 percent of the returns for the entire decade. So, if you were out of the stock market for those 10 days, you would have missed 40 percent of the returns for an entire decade. Since gains come quickly and unexpectedly, you can't afford to be on the sidelines.

186

- Buying and selling is costly, especially if your money isn't in a tax-sheltered plan. At the very least, you'll likely generate a big tax bill if you do a lot of trading.

The bottom line: Forget market timing, don't throw your money away on timing newsletters, and ignore the timing advice of investment gurus that you see on TV or hear on the radio. It's all snake oil.

There are prudent strategies you can implement to take advantage of the stock market's volatility. You might want to consider *dollar-cost averaging,* which is a fancy word for putting your money into the stock market (or possibly even the bond market) gradually instead of all at once. If you have a big chunk of your life savings to invest in the stock market, divide it by 12, 18, or even 24 and put an equal portion in each month over the course of 1 to 2 years. Why? If you invest a large amount all at once, you'd hate to have its value plunge shortly after you invest. Dollar-cost averaging is a tool to reduce that risk. The idea behind it is that you'll invest the same amount of money every month in hopes that the normal ups and downs of the stock market will result in a reduced average cost per share.

Here's how it's supposed to work. For illustration purposes, suppose you have $2000 and you choose to invest it over 5 months instead of all at once. Here's what might happen:

Dollar-Cost Averaging

Month	Amount Invested	Share Price	Shares Purchased
January	$ 400	$10	40
February	400	9	44.4
March	400	7	57.1
April	400	8	50
May	400	7	57.1
Total	$2000	$ 8.20 (average pr/sh)	248.6

Now here's what would have happened if you had invested everything at once. Ouch!

Lump Sum Investing

Month	Amount Invested	Share Price	Shares Purchased
January	$2000	$10	200

In the declining market laid out in the figure showing dollar-cost averaging, the use of dollar-cost averaging produces 248.6 shares at an average cost of $8.20 per share. But if you invest in one lump sum, you end up with only 200 shares and an average cost of $10 per share. By using dollar-cost averaging, your $2000 investment would be valued at $1740 in May (248.6 shares x $7/share). But if you'd have invested everything at once, as in the lump sum investing figure, your $2000 investment is worth only $1400 in May (200 shares x $7/share). Of course, this strategy won't enhance your return in a steadily rising market, but for most of us, it's better to be safe than sorry when investing big lump sums. Keep in mind that dollar-cost averaging won't work unless you're able to stay the course through thick and thin, both psychologically and financially. So make sure you have a 6- to 12-month emergency cash reserve and access to employment that will enable you to keep adding to your investments if you are dollar-cost averaging. And don't panic when the market plunges. Study the history of the stock market so you understand the importance of time in the market and the dangers of pulling out.

Most investors use dollar-cost averaging by default through monthly 401(k) payroll deductions, regular IRA contributions, and so forth. But as your holdings grow, eventually there comes a time when the impact of dollar-cost averaging diminishes. Monthly investments of $200 won't have much impact on a $300,000 portfolio. It's like a drop in the ocean. One way of dealing with that is to *rebalance your portfolio* at least annually to match your chosen asset allocation. If it is your intention to hold 50 percent stocks, 40 percent bonds, and 10 percent cash, you might find that you're actually holding 35 percent stocks, 50 percent bonds, and 15 percent cash after a steep stock market decline. Restoring your allocation will force you to buy stocks when stock prices are down, and sell bonds when bond prices are up. Selling high and buying low, that's what you'll be doing, and over time, it will work in your favor.

We're average, just like you, and when it comes to investing, average usually wins. Average families like ours will win by investing in index funds and earning average market returns. We'll win by implementing average buy/sell strategies like portfolio rebalancing and dollar-cost averaging. And we'll win by making sure that we're psychologically and financially prepared to stand firm and continue adding to our holdings during stock market declines, when everybody else is heading for the exits. If we can do these things, and there's no reason we can't, we'll leave most of the investment gurus in the dust. But the siren call of the market timers will always be there and a select few, probably by chance, will appear to have the magic. When they call out to you, remember the mousy, balding civil servant. Cover your ears, close your eyes, and ignore them.

DUMB MOVES

Our Investment Mistakes

We're going to 'fess up to some of the mistakes we've made with our investments. Most of these dumb moves were made when we were just getting started and have been corrected, but we suspect these are fairly common mistakes, so no laughing, pointing, or ridiculing please.

The Bill and Mary Hall of Shame

- *We wasted countless hours trying to find the best mutual funds.* All we ever found were the funds that did well in the past and they usually stopped being stellar performers when we put our money into them, as if the arrival of our money was their cue to become mediocre performers. It finally dawned on us that last year's chart toppers attract tons of cash and become hard to manage, especially when the fund's great performance probably had as much to do with luck as skill anyway. When the cash pours in and the manager's investment style goes out of favor, what have you got? A mediocre fund, that's what.

- *We listened to market timers.* Fortunately for us, the timer we followed remained bullish. But there were more bearish experts than bullish ones at the time and the bears were getting far more press, as they usually do, so we were just plain lucky that we didn't pull our money out of stocks. The bears didn't know what they were talking about, but now we know that the bulls didn't either. They were just lucky. And so were we.

- *When choosing mutual funds we focused 99 percent of our attention on returns and 1 percent on risks and expenses.* It should have been the other way around. Some top-performing mutual funds expose their investors to big risks. That's how they get those eye-popping returns. Furthermore, if your risky fund also has high expenses, the fund manager may be forced to take even more risks to offset those expenses. If you're paying him more, you expect him to put more money in your pocket, so he's under pressure to make up for the extra money you're paying him. He's likely to do that by taking even bigger risks.

- *We ignored the tax implications of investments in taxable accounts.* Mutual funds are required by law to pass on to their investors all the dividends and capital gains that the fund has realized throughout the year. Investors are required to pay any taxes owed on those gains in the year received. Now here's where it gets tricky:

  Most funds distribute gains in December so it doesn't make any sense to buy a fund right before a distribution. Wait until afterward so you won't incur a tax bill right away.

  The capital gains passed on to you by your mutual fund each year are created when the fund's manager sells some, but not all, of the holdings in the portfolio for more than he or she paid for them. When you sell shares of your fund or exchange them for shares of another fund, you're required to pay taxes on any capital gains that *you* incur (the difference between what you paid for the fund and your selling price). That's right, you'll pay taxes on the yearly capital gains distributed by the fund and you'll also pay on any gains that you generate by selling or exchanging your shares. How's that for another good reason to buy and hold?

- *We purchased no-load mutual funds through a discount brokerage's* No Transaction Fee *program.* NTF programs enable investors to buy no-load mutual funds from different companies under one roof, without paying transaction fees. Before NTF, if you wanted to own funds from four different companies, you had to deal with each company separately, which involved receiving a blizzard of statements. Transferring money from one company to another required the completion of forms and waiting for weeks or even months for the transfer to occur. With NTF programs, all you do is call the broker and transfers occur overnight; plus you get one consolidated statement that provides information on all your investments. Sounds pretty enticing, but there are some big disadvantages:

  First, our favorite mutual fund companies, Vanguard and USAA, don't participate. You can buy Vanguard and USAA funds through most NTF programs, but you must pay transaction fees.

  Second, the fund companies that do participate tend to charge higher annual expenses. They must do that so there's enough left over to reimburse the broker. Brokers handle all the paperwork, orders, and customer services and they won't do that for free.

  And finally, the NTF concept encourages trading because it's so easy to jump from one company's fund to another. Money invested in NTF programs has been referred to by some as "hot money." We don't want our money to be pooled with the money of investors more likely to do a lot of buying and selling because it drives up costs.

For these reasons, and personal experiences with very poor service at the NTF program we were using, we moved out of NTF funds altogether.

- *We followed the daily price movements of our investments.* Every day we'd record all the prices on little charts we carried with us. Why? I guess so we'd always have that information in case we needed it. Eventually it dawned on us that we never would. Now we download prices once per month and that's all we'll ever need. Watching prices every day serves no good purpose and feeds into a short-term, market-timing mindset, so why do it?

- *We owned too many funds.* Now we keep almost all of our investments in only five mutual funds: Vanguard Prime Money Market Fund; Vanguard Short-Term Bond Index Fund; Vanguard Total Bond Market Index Fund; Vanguard Total Stock Market Index Fund; Vanguard International Growth Fund. With most of our investments in index funds, we don't worry about mutual fund managers making big mistakes and losing our money, our investment expenses are minuscule, and record keeping is simple. In investing, that's about as good as it gets.

For us, investing used to be a hobby, almost a sport. We followed funds and their managers like sports fans follow teams and players. We watched our funds like chickens tend their eggs. We rejoiced when our funds did better than the market and despaired when they lagged. We've changed. Now investing is more like a business. We try to produce the most we can for the lowest cost and risk. We focus on issues we can control, like asset allocation, investment tax planning, and costs, and we ignore those things we can't control, like stock market price swings and finding top funds. We keep our emotions out of our investments as best we can. Investing is about avoiding mistakes and we've concluded that for us, buying and holding mostly index funds in an appropriate allocation is the closest we can possibly come to avoiding mistakes. We'll never be famous investors and we can't brag about huge returns, but our lives are at stake here, and that's a very serious business. We just can't afford to make mistakes. It's not a hobby anymore.

PART NINE

RETIREMENT

I was shooting the breeze a while back with a 65-year-old coworker. He was a few weeks away from retirement and was telling me about a chat he had with a lady in our personnel office. She told him that he would love retirement. When he asked her how she knew that, she said, "Because retirees I knew when they were still working come here to conduct business and they seem different. They look more relaxed and peaceful. Plus, they tell me they're happy and I believe them." We believe them, too. But retiring early poses some special issues and risks that we discuss in the following section.

PLANS

IRAs, Roths, 403(b)s, 401(k)s, SIMPLES, SEPs, Keoghs . . .

For most families, there are only four big tax breaks: deductible mortgage interest, higher education tax credits, child tax credits, and tax-deferred retirement plans. The best, by far, are the tax-deferred retirement plans, but two flaws tend to scare people away from these terrific tax savers.

1. *Lockup.* We're always hearing in the media that most families spend every dime they earn, so it's not surprising that many shy away from plans that lock up their money until retirement. When you're young, have children to support, and you're living from check to check, it's tough to set aside any money and it can be terrifying to put your money where it is essentially out of reach. And calling them "retirement plans" doesn't help. With kids to raise, lives to live, and jobs to do, who has time to deal with retirement?

2. *Complexity.* Our congressional representatives have really stuck it to us. These retirement plans are staggeringly complex. Ask your accountant or your lawyer and if they're

straight with you, they'll admit that most general practice attorneys and accountants don't understand employer-sponsored tax-deferred retirement plans. And this problem is magnified by the horribly written IRS publications that are supposed to guide us through the maze. I challenge anyone to determine the maximum deduction allowed in a 403(b) on the basis of information provided in IRS Publication 571. If you turn to the IRS for help, don't expect much. I recently asked their Tax Law Assistance office to tell me the deadline for making a SIMPLE IRA contribution. All I wanted was a date. They wouldn't provide that information but they did say this, ". . . you will need to research in the private sector. The Internal Revenue Service does not administer pension plans, but deals with the tax consequences related to them. . . ." In other words, they won't help honest taxpayers get it right, but they'll hammer you if you get it wrong.

Despite these flaws, we believe in retirement plans and use them extensively. The bottom line is this: If you want financial freedom you must use retirement plans. These plans can more than double your life savings in two ways. First, they free up money for investing that would have been spent on taxes. For example, in 1998 we put over $17,000 into retirement plans and that's $17,000 we'd have paid taxes on if we hadn't used those plans. Second, investments in retirement plans are sheltered from taxes until withdrawn, so if we make a killing in the financial markets, we aren't taxed on all those dividends and capital gains until we withdraw the money. In 1998 we had $8750 in interest, dividends, and realized capital gains that were generated inside our retirement plans. If those investments weren't sheltered in retirement plans, we'd have paid taxes on that $8750. And since we plan to live quite simply when we retire, it's likely we'll never pay taxes on a large portion of our investment returns. But in 1998 alone we avoided taxes on $25,750; retirement plan contributions accounted for more than $17,000, and sheltered dividends and gains generated inside our retirement plans from contributions made in prior years accounted for another $8750. So our tax saving in 1998 was a cool $7386. That's right, we'd have paid at least an additional $7386 in taxes in 1998 without our retirement plans. Average low- to middle-income families like ours just can't afford to ignore these plans. But what about the insecurity that goes along with locking up our money for so long? We believe that if you adopt the strategies in this book, limited access to money in your retirement plans won't be much of an issue. Here's why:

- We advocate saving at such a high rate that you'll be building taxable investments while also contributing the maximum to retirement plans. We put almost as much into our taxable investment accounts as we do into our retirement plans and if you do that, you'll have so much in your taxable accounts within a few years that you'll never worry about needing to access the money in your retirement plans.

- We advocate that every family should have an emergency cash reserve sufficient to cover 6–12 months of living expenses.

- We advocate a reasonably comfortable life at a dramatically reduced cost, so if you're living on 60 percent of your income and saving the other 40 percent, the loss of one job won't be a catastrophe if the other spouse is working. You're probably living off only one income anyway.

- We advocate visualizing money in terms of the income it can produce, not the things it will buy. If in your mind's eye you can picture your money as your replacement in the workforce, the thought of raiding your retirement accounts will make you cringe.

- We advocate the use of substantially equal periodic payments to access retirement account funds without penalty before age $59\frac{1}{2}$. Although you won't be able to access all your money at once, you can withdraw some of it on a regular basis, without penalty. We discuss this in more detail in the next chapter.

The ins and outs of retirement plans can be terribly complex. What can honest taxpayers do to get it right? Of course, you'll want to study the rules so you have a working knowledge of the system and we suggest some resources in another chapter. But when you're stumped, we have found that large no-load mutual fund companies such as Vanguard (1-800-662-7447) and USAA (1-800-531-8777) have retirement plan specialists on staff who are truly knowledgeable. They know far more than most general practice accountants and lawyers and they'll provide information for free. If you have a 403(b), USAA will even perform a complex calculation (the calculation is several pages long!) that will tell you the maximum amount you can deduct, and they'll do that for you each year for free. Both companies have an extensive library of literature they'll mail to you free of charge. Vanguard's website (www.vanguard.com) is loaded with well-written, understandable information about retirement plans. So don't worry too much about the complexity. Help is available through toll-free numbers, extensive libraries of free literature, and websites that are jam packed with good information.

If you're just getting started, sign up at work for any retirement plan employer matches you're eligible to receive before you contribute to other plans or accelerate mortgage payments. Next, access any other unmatched workplace retirement plans (401(k), 403(b), SIMPLE IRA, SEP IRA, 457 Plans, etc.) and contribute the maximum allowed. If you're also making mortgage payments, we'd suggest that you max your retirement plans and accelerate the house payments at the same time unless there is an employer match, which should always be your first choice. If you can't afford to do both, compare your mortgage rate (after subtracting federal and state tax breaks) to rates on investments like triple A rated corporate bonds, CDs, and Treasuries. If you can't get more than 1 or 2 percent extra in these types of investments, pay off the mortgage. Be careful, though. You don't want to get into a situation where you never save for retirement due to high mortgage payments. If you're in that fix, *get a smaller house!*

After you've contributed the maximum to your plans at work, put up to $2,000 per spouse into an IRA. You'll need to decide whether to go with a traditional IRA or a Roth IRA. That decision requires a calculator and a crystal ball, but if you plan to pursue the strategies in this book it will probably serve your interests to put anything you can deduct into a traditional IRA, and the balance into a Roth IRA. That's what we do because we expect to be in a lower tax bracket when we start living off our assets, and it's possible that we won't pay any taxes at all on most of our IRA withdrawals. So we take any deduction we can get now in hopes that we'll avoid taxation altogether in the future. Generally speaking, a Roth IRA is probably better for people whose tax bracket will rise or stay the same when they start withdrawing from it. Another small consideration: There have been some concerns that the Roth IRA might be accessible to creditors in some states. Traditional IRAs and other retirement plans often aren't, but it depends on your state. Potential protection from creditors! How's that for another reason to put as much as you can into retirement plans? For more information, check out an article in *Lawyers Weekly USA* at www.lawyers weekly.com/featira2.htm, and for general information about Roth IRAs, refer to www.rothira.com.

Setting up an IRA is a breeze. Call the mutual fund and ask for an IRA packet. When it arrives, fill out the application. I have one in front of me now. It requests your name, address, social security number, birth date, and phone number. Plus you'll need to tell them what fund to put your money in, which tax year the contribution applies to, and who should get the account if you die. That's it! Enclose a check in the postage-paid envelope they provide, drop it in the mail, and you're done. Easy!

We go against conventional wisdom and put our stock investments in retirement plans and our bonds in our taxable accounts. Most experts recommend doing the opposite. The thinking is that the bonds generate more taxable earnings (interest and dividends) while stock dividends are often only half as much or less and stock capital gains are minimal if you buy and hold (capital gains are simply the difference between what you paid for the stock or stock mutual fund and what you sold it for). It might make sense in theory to hold stocks and stock mutual funds, especially stock index funds, in your taxable accounts, but we don't follow conventional wisdom for three reasons:

1. Our retirement plans are essentially locked up and unavailable for our use until needed in retirement. If we put our stock holdings in our taxable accounts, those accounts won't be accessible either because we'd likely incur a huge capital gains tax bill if we liquidate those funds. We don't want to get into a situation where all of our money is inaccessible if that can be avoided.

2. Putting stock mutual funds into taxable accounts restricts our ability to sell a bad fund and buy a better one. If we sell one fund because it's a loser and buy another, we're likely to incur a big capital gains tax bill when we sell. We prefer to have complete flexibility with our stock holdings because they pose more risk.

3. Capital gains tax rules are rather complex and continually changing. Since we're more likely to encounter substantive capital gains issues with stock funds, we prefer to keep them in retirement plans where those gains aren't taxed until withdrawn. It's just easier at tax time.

Retirement plans are far more complex than they need to be, but they're still the best thing since sliced bread for low- to middle-income families. If you aren't using them, tape this note to your forehead:

To Do Tomorrow

- Go to personnel office and sign up for my company's 401(k).
- Call a mutual fund and get IRA application.

- Ask mutual fund to send educational literature on retirement plans.

Just remember to remove the note from your forehead before you walk into your personnel office tomorrow. Retirement plans are great, but they aren't much good unless you have a job where you can earn money to put into them.

WITHDRAWING

Getting Your Money Out of Retirement Plans Whenever You Want—Without Penalties

The idea behind retirement plans is to provide a way for regular folks like us to set some money aside for our golden years without worrying about the ravages of taxation on our retirement stash. And if you think about it, it really is in the nation's interest to provide that system. If we didn't, we'd probably all be living in poverty when we're old. We don't want that for our parents or for ourselves. So, our elected representatives put together a patchwork of retirement programs with eligibility requirements and contribution rules so complex that most rocket scientists would break down in tears of frustration if they tried to make sense of them. An accountant told me a few days ago that retirement plan compliance is so poor due to lack of understanding, that the IRS isn't likely to crack down on individual investors or small employers. Another accountant told me that most general practice accountants and attorneys don't have a clue about the ins and outs of retirement plans. It's a huge mess that's been swept under the rug and everybody knows it. Every single one of these plans should be scrapped and replaced with one plan accessible to every citizen, but that isn't likely to happen with all the other pressing issues.

Fortunately, Congress did provide an escape hatch; a way to get to your retirement plan money without any penalties at any time you choose to do so. Actually, there are several escape hatches but most of them are worthless to most of us. For example, in a traditional IRA you can get your money out to pay for medical expenses that exceed 7.5 percent of your adjusted gross income. Who cares? If you're spending more than 7.5 percent of your income on medical expenses, it probably means you have someone with serious health problems and you don't have health insurance. Raiding your retirement plan to pay for health care will only compound your problems. Another example: you can pull out up to $10,000 to buy your first home. Big deal! Most young people aren't going to mess around with an IRA for two or three years to save for a down payment on a house. Or, how about this one? You can raid your retirement plans to pay for health insurance if you lose your job. Of course, you probably won't have access to any health insurance if you lose your job, but hey, just in case you luck out, you're all set. Why didn't Congress give us access to our retirement money for food or shelter if we lose our jobs? I guess they think it's not too bad to starve or freeze as long as we have access to treatment for those conditions. What a bunch of geniuses!

Well, they did get one thing right. They created a way to access money in retirement plans without penalties *before* age 59½ and you can use the money to live on. It's called *substantial equal periodic payments*. The concept is simple. You take out just enough each year to deplete the IRA by the time you are expected to die. Since you have no way of knowing when you'll die or how your investments will perform in the interim, you use life expectancy tables and reasonable interest rate assumptions as approved by the IRS. It sounds complicated, and it is, but it works. Depending on your age and which of the general assumptions you use, you'll be able to withdraw roughly 3 percent to 8 percent of your investments per year, and the process is flexible enough to enable you to choose the method that will let you get your hands on an amount that's right for you. Once you start the process, you must continue these withdrawals for 5 years or until age 59½, whichever is *later*. If you screw it up, they'll hammer you, so this isn't something for the do-it-yourselfer. You'll definitely want to use an accountant to help set it up, if you can find one who knows how.

These rules don't apply to Roth IRAs. With the Roth, you'll be penalized for withdrawals made within 5 years or before age 59½. Maybe they'll let you tap your Roth for the hair transplant you're likely to need from pulling it out trying to keep all these rules straight.

ENOUGH

Keeping Our Money from Petering Out Before We Do

M ost of us who have full-time jobs don't worry too much about the source of our pay because we have relatively stable employers who pay us consistently. But when we're living off our investments, it's up to us to ensure that our assets won't run out before we die. Because the value of our holdings will fluctuate, there is no way to know how long they'll last.

Most of us who have full-time jobs don't worry too much about inflation because our employers usually boost our pay on an annual basis, so the pay we get this year will buy as much as the pay we got last year. But when we're living off our assets, nobody is going to step in and give us a raise. We need to plan for that. We need to provide those raises to ourselves. But there is no way to know in advance how much these inflation-generated pay raises will cost because we don't know how high (or low) inflation will go.

If we don't know how our stocks and bonds will perform over the next 50 years or what inflation will do, how can we possibly determine what we'll need to cover our expenses over a long period of time with so many variables to contend with? It's a tough question. We'll walk through our personal situation and show you how we've dealt with it.

On the expense side of the ledger, we plan to live on about $2250 per month. Each of us wants to work about 10 hours per week, which should bring in about $780 per month, and that's if we earn only $9 per hour, which we should be able to exceed easily. That leaves $1470 that our assets will need to produce. We own our house free and clear, have no other debts, and have roughly $407,000 invested in stocks, bonds, and cash. Is that enough? Have we achieved our goal?

Some experts suggest that an annual spending rate of somewhere between 4 percent and 5 percent of a 50/50 stock/bond portfolio should last indefinitely. There have been a few worst-case scenarios in this century, however, where investors spending 5 percent were hit with high inflation and/or a severe market decline in the first years of their retirement and those folks would have outlived their assets. Nevertheless, a spending rate of 4 percent is considered to be very conservative and a 5 percent rate of spending is common for endowment funds of institutions like universities and museums. We plan to spend 5 percent of our assets adjusted annually for inflation. But we can't just ignore those historical worst-case scenarios, so we plan to add these additional safeguards:

- We will set aside $50,000 in a short-term bond mutual fund, like Vanguard's Short-Term Bond Index Fund. We'll use that to cover our living expenses if we encounter a brutal bear market and/or high inflation in the early years. That $50,000 should cover us for about 3 years and help to minimize the impact of an early catastrophe. It will replace the $25,000 cash reserve that we hold now for emergencies.

- We believe inflation is overstated and that we'll be able to lower our own inflation rate. For example, we can live without orange juice until the prices return to normal after an early freeze in Florida. The Consumer Price Index assumes we won't. We'll hunt for super bargains. The Consumer Price Index assumes we won't. We plan to trim about 1 percent off the official rate of inflation, so if the official rate is 3 percent, we'll boost our annual withdrawal by only 2 percent. You need to be aware, however, that the government does occasionally adjust the way consumer prices are calculated. For example, there was a slight adjustment effective January 1999 that is estimated to reduce the inflation rate by two-tenths of 1 percent. So it's a good idea to check the web page of the Bureau of Labor Statistics every year or two (http://stats.bls.gov). Also keep in mind that the official rate of inflation is likely to be different from your own; it's only a rough estimate.

- We'll roll with the punches. When the experts determine sustainable withdrawal rates, and suggest a 4 percent or 5 percent rate with caveats about worst-case scenarios, they're operating in a theoretical world where numbers are fed into a computer. But computers don't consider the fact that we have a brain. The computer assumes that if we get clobbered with high inflation and/or a punishing bear market, we'll just keep right on selling our holdings at rock bottom prices to pay our bills. But smart people get off the tracks if a train is coming. If needed, we'll tighten our belts or increase our work hours, and maybe even do things like plant a garden in addition to the previous safeguards. We'll bob, weave, duck, run, or whatever we need to do. We can do that. We're smart. So are you.

A 5 percent withdrawal rate with a few extra safeguards should minimize the impact of historical worst-case scenarios. Of course, no one knows what the future holds, and it could be worse than anything we've ever seen, but that's not likely. If it happens, we'll deal with it, but the odds are with us.

So, in the first year we'll withdraw 5 percent of our portfolio balance and in subsequent years we'll change the dollar amount of our withdrawals by the rate of inflation of the previous year. For example, if we assume for illustration purposes, that inflation is 2 percent and our investments have a total return of 8 percent after the first year of our financial freedom, the process would work like this:

- If Mary and I initiated our plan today, we'd start the first year with $407,000.
- Next, we'd subtract $50,000 and put that into a short-term bond fund to be used in the event of a bear market and/or high inflation in the early years. Now we have $357,000.
- Then we'd subtract 5 percent of the $357,000 ($17,850) to live on during the first year. We're left with $339,150.
- If our $339,150 balance earns 8 percent during the first year, we end that year with $366,282.
- At the start of year number two we'd withdraw $18,029, which is what we withdrew last year ($17,850) plus last year's 2 percent inflation rate (reduced to 1 percent because we believe that inflation rates are overstated). We're left with $348,253.
- If our $348,253 earns 7.5 percent during the second year, we end that year with $374,372.

Subsequent years would be handled in the same manner; simply withdraw the same dollar amount as the previous year, plus the rate of inflation (after adjusting the official inflation rate downward by 1 percent to reflect your incredible spending prowess). That's all there is to it.

So have Mary and I made it? Have we reached our goal? Well, we need $2250 per month and we'll each work about 10 hours a week, which should net about $780 per month, to be replaced by social security and Medicare eventually. We'll set aside $50,000 in a short-term bond fund as a safeguard against the worst. We'll invest the $357,000 balance and spend 5 percent per year which is about $1488 per month. Work produces $780 and our assets should produce $1488 for a total of $2268 per month. So, yes, we're there; exactly where we want to be. The grass is very green here. Join us. You can do it.

THREATS

A Sample of Things That Can Go Wrong

If you've had any investment experience, you've seen statements like this: "The fund's past performance should not be viewed as indicative of future returns." In other words, nobody has a clue what the future has in store for the financial markets. Things could go wrong, even terribly wrong. It's not difficult to envision scenarios in which some national or global tragedy wipes out one's assets or makes them worthless: things like a great depression, war, pestilence, hyperinflation, transfer of power to political extremists, and countless other doomsday scenarios. Yet, the world is a better place to live in than it has ever been before and the rate of improvement seems to be growing exponentially, so we aren't terribly worried about cataclysmic disasters. What we do worry about are more likely threats. Things like these:

- "Mom? Dad? I have bad news. Tom will die without treatment but it will cost at least $150,000. We don't have health insurance and I have nowhere else to turn. I am so sorry to ask you, but I can't let him die. He's my husband and I love him. You love him, too. My children need their father. Help us, please."

The health-care distribution system in this country is still a mess despite some tinkering around the edges accomplished through Kennedy/Kassebaum legislation at the federal level and individual state initiatives. The ongoing lack of health care security is a national disgrace and stands as the biggest threat to the financial freedom of average families.

Lately politicians have been blabbering about initiating some more minor changes to get a few more children covered by health insurance. Covering children but not their parents; what a bunch of dim bulbs. We live in the richest land in history and should have access to affordable health care for all. It's doable. Unfortunately, average families can't afford to buy politicians. Insurance companies can. In Iowa, we're able to buy insurance without regard to preexisting conditions but prices are high. So we'll pay those high prices and hope for the best.

We don't have any good answers to this problem. There is a terrific website, broken down by state, where you can check the minimal protections that apply to you: (www.georgetown.edu/research/ihcrp/hipaa/). Beyond doing our best to understand the system, all we can do is hope for health-care reform and vote against politicians who stand in the way. Until the mess is fixed it's every man, woman, and child for himself.

- We're in a global economy whether we like it or not. Although the world will likely be better for it in the long run, many families have been and will be hurt by the export of jobs to Third World countries.

For the individual, education is the only hope. Unfortunately, little is being done to assist dislocated workers. Funding for good programs like Workforce Development and the Job Training

Partnership Act (JTPA) is insufficient and new educational tax breaks fall far short of what's needed to retrain workers whose careers have been shipped overseas. If you're in a low paid, unskilled job, education is your ticket out. It will be the best investment you'll ever make.

- We hear a lot about the demise of social security and Medicare and we're probably in for some nasty changes, like extended eligibility dates that are more in line with life expectancies. How does working until you're 80 sound?

We're counting on social security retirement benefits to replace our part-time work, so we're hoping they'll choose a better solution, like investing some of the Social Security Trust Fund in stock index funds. Currently, the trust fund is invested 100 percent in Treasury securities. If a financial planner did that to you as an individual, he could probably be sued for incompetence. Private university and hospital trust funds invest in stocks and so do government employee pension plans. Why not social security?

- We've been so busy working and accumulating a nest egg that we haven't delved into the intricacies of long-term care insurance.

We'll be turning to that subject soon as we prepare to leave our full-time jobs. Nursing home care isn't very exciting to think about, but if ignored, it could be our eventual financial undoing. So, we'll be ready, even if it means working for another year or so now to pay for the long-term care we may need in the future.

- Frequent relocations due to layoffs, downsizing, or even promotions, can be quite expensive and emotionally draining. There are moving expenses, utility hook-up fees, double mortgage payments until the former house is sold, decorating costs, and so on.

The temptation to dip into retirement plans to cover such costs must be overwhelming and at times unavoidable. When we chose our jobs we didn't have a clue what we were doing. We were simply lucky to have obtained jobs that would last more than two decades. If you're planning ahead and want a job that's likely to last, take a job with an organization that has been around for a long time and one that has a whole passel of employees with 20 years or more on the job.

- We started investing in 1991 and have had mostly an up market ever since. We could encounter a severe, protracted bear market, the likes of which has never been seen before.

That isn't likely but it's possible and the only impenetrable shield is to stay out of investments that go up and down in price. Problem is, if you do that you aren't likely to reach your goals because much of your paltry returns will be wiped out by inflation and taxes and there won't be enough left to live on. If you're able to live on roughly $3\frac{1}{2}$ percent of your investments annually, consider putting every penny you have into Treasury Inflation-Indexed Securities. If the economy comes completely unglued, we'll envy you. Unfortunately, most of us won't be able to achieve financial freedom unless we keep a portion of our money in the stock and bond markets.

There are no guarantees in the realm of investing but the odds are with us and the world is getting safer, better, and smarter every day. All we can do is try as best we can to avoid mistakes and hope for the best. If we do that, most of us will succeed. Seizing control of our destinies, recapturing our time, and changing our lives—it's worth the risks.

PART TEN

PARENTING

Do you think kids are cheap? Think again. According to *U.S. News and World Report*, it costs about 1.45 million dollars to support a typical child from conception through college.* Obviously, most of us are getting the job done for much less. And if you really think about it, it's probably far better for our children if we don't spend so much money on them, because earning all that money consumes time that might be better spent with our children. Have you noticed that some of those school shooting sprees have occurred in wealthy neighborhoods? Until recently, we didn't have much money to spend on our kids, so we gave them our time instead and that has worked well for us. They've survived just fine and we've been able to pack away almost a half-million dollars while raising them. If you're spending a million and a half on each child, you might want to consider doing it for a fraction of that. Here's how we did it.

*P. Longman, "The Cost of Children," *U.S. News & World Report*, March 30, 1998, pp. 51–53, 56–58.

SUPPER

We Raise Our Kids at Dinner

Dinner is where we get to know our kids. It's where we build our relationships with our children and infuse them with our values. Dinner is where we hear about everyone's day and discuss problems we've encountered. It's where we support each other, laugh, and sometimes cry. Most parents love their kids but do they really *like* them? We do; and we learned to like them at dinner.

Dinner is where we raise our children. Think about it. In the morning most of us sleep until we have just enough time to make it to work. Barely. Then we come home in the evening and we have dinner. After that there's dishes, homework, various activities, and that all-important flop time. Then it's off to bed. If we don't eat with our kids, they're probably raising themselves.

So what does all this have to do with money? Three things:

1. When families don't eat together, it is usually because they have other important activities to attend: sports, church, civic, social, or whatever. Most of those activities cost money. There are miles on the car, uniforms, admission fees, restaurant bills,

and so on. If you work all day and continue with more activities in the evening, you're more likely to buy fast food, use a dry cleaner, hire a cleaning service, or pay someone to mow your lawn or do your taxes. So we're going to suggest something that might not be popular, but here goes: Avoid organized sports, civic involvement, and church activities, especially when your children are under age twelve. Saving money is only part of it. Your children need you to build their character and you can't do that if you aren't there to talk to them every day for an hour or so. One of our area banks ran a television advertisement that touted the virtues of one of their managers. It showed him on a mat teaching wrestling to a group of about 20 boys. We're supposed to love that bank because its employees really care about our community, but we wonder if the world would be a better place if all the businesses out there just let their employees stay home and spend time with their own kids rather than sending them out to save everyone else's. There's no better gift to the community than good kids who become wonderful young adults.

2. If you spend time with your children at dinner, you'll receive daily progress reports on their academic performance. When problems crop up, you'll be on top of them right away. Your children will be better students because you've helped them work through some inevitable academic difficulties, and because they know that you value good performance in school. This will translate into college scholarships and, hopefully, adult children who actually get jobs and leave home.

3. You'll learn about your children's peers at dinner, and over time you'll learn who the rats are. If you're hashing all this out at dinner every evening, your kids will learn to identify the bad apples and they'll develop an aversion to their antics. They will also be more likely to stay away from the delinquents, and if they do, you could save a ton of money on sub-

stance abuse counseling, teen pregnancy, smashed up cars and injured bodies, and damage to your home (like wild parties when you are gone). Trust us on this one. We both work on the front lines in human services occupations. There's far more pain and heartache out there than most people realize.

So, the next time you get pressured to join some church committee or civic organization that's trying to save the world, ask yourself if you're having dinner with your kids. If you aren't, do your family and your community a big favor and say "No." The world and all its problems will still be waiting for you in a few years, but your kids won't.

INDULGE

Spending Money on Kids

Childhood isn't what it used to be. When we were kids, our parents knew what we were up to, for the most part, but it was actually possible in those days to do something rotten without getting caught, because there were times when neither Mom nor Dad were right by our sides. In fact, there must have been plenty of times, because I can remember lots of crummy things we did, especially when cousins came to visit. Cousins were great. They'd come to visit us on our northwest Iowa farm from faraway places (like southwest Iowa) and teach us all kinds of sinister things we wouldn't have thought of ourselves. I suppose they'd say the same about us; at least, I hope they would. The point is, the World War II/Korean War generation of parents weren't doting over us all the time. We had time to play with our peers, to make mistakes, and to have fun on our own. And when we screwed up, they'd let us have it. It seemed to work well. They had it just about right.

These days family life revolves around the kids' activities and children are the center of the family. Organized sports run year round for kids from 4 to 18. There is even a term for it: *soccer moms,* a generation of young women defined by their children and the organized sports they play. Today parents spend their free time hovering over their sons and daughters and live out their young adult lives immersed in children's activities.

When we were growing up, children shared a room (or a bed) with siblings. There was one TV in the living room and a radio in the kitchen. Most of us had our own bike, some sporting equipment, and whatever toys we got for Christmas and birthdays. But that's changed in many homes today. A few days ago one of our daughters overheard a schoolmate say, "I'm spoiled and that's fine. My sister and I get anything we want and I don't see anything wrong with that." Have you noticed all the little kids wearing designer clothes these days? It isn't unusual to see $200 worth of clothes on an 8-year-old who also has a private bedroom decked out with TV, VCR, stereo, and enough toys to open a store. Things have changed.

Have you been to a college campus recently? When we attended private colleges back in the early 1970s, very few students had cars. We walked. Now college parking lots are jammed. And take a look at some of the new apartment buildings these ritzy colleges build. Most parents of the students living in those apartments probably couldn't afford to rent equivalent quarters.

Every 3 or 4 years our local high school band takes a trip. They might go to Chicago or Minneapolis to take in a professional basketball game, tour the big city, and stay over for a night or two. The kids have a good time. There are some costs involved, maybe a couple hundred or so, but not much. This year they're pushing a trip to Hawaii and each child needs to come up with $1200. Not to worry, the promotional flyers say. The money can be earned over time; there's no rush to produce the cash now. Sign up now and pay later for this "ONCE IN A LIFETIME OPPORTUNITY!" Why Hawaii? "Why not?!" touts the literature.

Several years ago our daughter won a trip to Europe in a cheerleading contest, but the term "won" was used very loosely. She would need to pay for the trip. "Can I please go, Mom? . . . Dad? . . . No? . . . Why not?"

Here's why not:

- Kids who have everything don't have much to look forward to or work toward. Nothing can compete with what they're used to having. When parents set them on a velvet cushion and attend to their every whim for 18 years, and then send them off to college where they accumulate staggering debts, and graduate into low-paying jobs and tiny apartments, we set them up to be miserable. Life is a disappointment for them. Is it any wonder that so many young adults return to live with Mom and Dad, or that we hear on the news that alarming numbers of graduating college students file for bankruptcy?

- Teens about to go to college have no business buying trips to Europe, trips to Hawaii, cars, or other big ticket items. If they do, there's a good chance they'll end up paying for these expenditures by borrowing more for college later. In other words, they'll pay for the Hawaii trip today with additional money they'll borrow for college in the future. Children can't completely grasp the concept of debt. So we help them by saying *No* when they ask to spend all their earnings on exotic trips, cars, and other expensive luxuries. We help them to lay the groundwork for their own financial security. It's a gift.

Rosemary Toohey (my mother) grew up during the Great Depression and recalls her childhood in a children's story she wrote in 1992. The story is entitled "Holding." Here's what she said:

Do you have something special you like to touch or hold? When I was a young girl I had two things very special to me. My mother's coat and my dog, Tippy. . . .

After school we had our favorite programs we would listen to on the radio, like you have on television. I would go into the living room, lie down on the davenport and my mother would cover me with her coat to keep me toasty warm. It was a new coat, but Mother didn't mind. The special thing about her coat was that it was lined with fur. How wonderful it was to hold the coat over me and snuggle under it. I would listen to my program and always fall asleep before it ended. I would awaken to the smell of fresh fried potatoes with ground black pepper that we were having for supper.

At night, our bedrooms were cold and unheated. . . . I had a favorite puppy; warm, soft, furry Tippy, who would crawl under the covers with my sister and me. I would cuddle and hold her close to me. We were both happy. . . . When we awoke, Mother had oatmeal made for breakfast and we used lots of milk on it in a bowl or sometimes in a cup so we could drink it if we were in a hurry. Then off to school, running and knowing I had my mother's new fur-lined coat and soft, warm Tippy waiting at home for me. I was very happy.

We must do a better job of making our kids feel like that. It costs us a fortune to indulge our children, but it costs them even more.

DISCIPLINE

Chaos Poses a Threat to Your Family's Financial Health

No one wants to raise a brat. Then why are there so many of them? We think it's because the notion of indulging kids was hot in pop psychology a couple of decades ago and it spilled over into the media where it has been perpetuated. Many parents really believe that children are the center of the family and the family revolves around them. They also think that children should not be allowed to experience frustration. We disagree.

There was an ad on TV awhile back; maybe you remember it. In the foreground you see this mother talking about her "cuddly wuddly ray of sunshine" or something like that. In the background you see a 5- or 6-year-old frolicking in the meadow while sucking down some juice that this ad is peddling. But Mom has a dilemma. The juice is full of vitamins that are good for the child and this savvy mother ponders whether she should tell her angel that the juice is good for her. She gives us viewers a knowing and conspiratorial look and declares something like, "Why tell her and risk losing one of these rare tantrum-free moments?"

So here we have a corporation that thinks it can connect with juice-buying moms by portraying this demanding and controlling child as lovable and by representing the mother as ineffective and wisely resigned to her impotence. The whole scene appears to have been designed to be cute and we were all supposed to think, "Boy, I can sure relate to that." Sorry, juice company, but it isn't cute or funny. The whole subject of raising little kids is serious stuff for many reasons, one of the least of which is financial. Yes, that's right. Poorly behaved kids cost more money. Here are just a few of the reasons why:

- In child-centered families, the parents communicate less, causing stress in the relationship. The kids direct the conversation. We've all seen this. Dad can be talking to Mom and little Suzy enters and says something irrelevant. The conversation stops until Mom hears Suzy out. By the time she's done, Dad has probably left the room. Loving couples fall out of love in child-centered families. Unhappy people spend money to feel better. And really, really unhappy people get divorced, which is financial Armageddon.

- Unruly children don't do well in school, which means that college scholarships won't be granted in the future. We're talking thousands and thousands in extra college costs and interest on student loans.

- Families ruled by children are often chaotic. Parents have no time to think, to plan, or to learn how to save and invest money. We've seen families where the kids aren't put to bed until 11:00 or 12:00 at night! The parents can't even get enough sleep to function in their jobs.

- Kids who are out of control damage property. They eat (and spill) in the living room. They track mud into the house. They jump on things and throw things and break things. Then you pay to replace what they break. We've seen nice homes that were so trashed it would have been cheaper to bring in a bull-dozer and start over than to fix the place.

So what should you do? We follow six guidelines that have helped make for smoother sailing:

1. *No spanking or hitting.* Why? Well, lots of reasons, but primar-ily this: It doesn't work! If it did there wouldn't be so many lit-tle holy terrors out there. There's no worse environment for a child than a child-centered family where the kids are indulged, doted upon, and the center of attention. Eventually there will be a meltdown and the parents will resort to the final line of defense: brute force. They have no alternative because the kids become intolerable. But such parents have probably lost the battle and their only escape is to wait for their tikes to grow up and move away.

2. *No anger allowed when disciplining.* Your child may react emo-tionally when challenged. You shouldn't. If you do you'll place yourself on the same level as your child. One of you needs to be an adult. That would be you.

3. *No caving in to the child's resistance to authority.* Children are a work in progress. When they're born they are like a lump of clay, and it is our job as parents to mold and sculpt them. You can't give in to their resistance because they don't know what they are doing. You do. They can't possibly grasp the "big pic-ture." You can.

4. *Discipline with confidence and love.* It is your job as parents to give the world a good and decent person. So when your 2-, 3-, or 4-year-old does something rotten, you simply take her by the shoulders, look straight into her eyes, and say, "No." But you must know with absolute certainty that it will be "No." You must believe it completely. There can be no doubt in your eyes, in your voice, or in your gentle but firm grip on her shoulders. You are saying, feeling, and knowing "No" with your whole being and you're doing it for a very high pur-

pose—you are teaching your child to be a good person. You are doing it for your child, your family, and for your community. There is no nobler cause, no higher calling. It is a mission of love. Children recognize and respond to confidence. You're wielding the incredible power of love and they usually won't resist it. If you discipline with confidence when they're little, you won't have problems when they're older. By age 5 you'll be essentially done.

5. *Time out.* Occasionally your little one will challenge your authority even if you discipline with confidence and love. They will either throw a tantrum, go limp when you try to remove them from a situation, or just look at you and say "No." Our youngest, Meghann, was a master of those things until age 4 or 5. When she got out of hand we'd just isolate her for 2 or 3 minutes in her room. We'd calmly tell her she could scream and cry "in here" where it wouldn't bother the rest of us and that she could come out when she was done. With no audience she'd finish in 2 or 3 minutes and when she came out, we'd discuss the issue again. Worked every time. Meghann is now one of the nicest young ladies we've ever known.

6. *Present a united front.* We have a plaque on the wall in our home that says, "The most important thing a father can do for his children is to love their mother." The reverse is also true. Don't let your kids pit one of you against the other. When both parents, always in love, unite in a mission to raise good and decent sons and daughters, they can't lose.

Well-behaved kids mean peaceful homes and a better world, but they also produce big savings on college expenses, repair bills, and impulse buying. Getting this part of your family's life in order results in big payoffs for everyone.

EXPECTATIONS

Setting High Expectations for Children Without Driving Them Crazy

The bell rang and our youngest child, Meghann, was hustling through the crowded hall with only 2 minutes until her next class. When you're in sixth grade you don't want to be noticed, so straggling into your classroom after everyone is already seated and quiet is unthinkable. Getting to class on time while avoiding eighth graders en route are matters of life and death to 12-year-olds. As Meggie was weaving through the crowd, a fellow sixth grader strayed into the path of one of those evil eighth graders and his armful of books and papers were unceremoniously dumped onto the floor and scattered over a wide area by a hundred hurrying feet. Meggie stopped and helped him pick up a couple books. No big deal. The whole thing took 10 seconds, tops, and off she went. Forgotten. Except that a teacher who had observed it called Meggie into her room, praised her, and rewarded her with candy. She told us about it at supper that night and we got into quite a discussion. In the end, we all agreed that while her small act of kindness was a nice thing to do, it fell into the category of "expectations." She would be expected to help a peer in a situation like that. She didn't exceed our expectations. She met them.

Here's another example. Right now, as I write this, I'm holding in my hand a "Certificate of Award" signed by Meghann's middle school principal. It looks like a college diploma. Very impressive. But it's for handing in her classroom assignments on a regular basis. Isn't she required to do that?

What about this one? Have you noticed all the parents these days who come to church with 5- and 6-year-olds who seem to need a bag of storybooks, toys, and little containers of cereal to get through the 1-hour service? There's no expectation that they'll behave unless entertained. And how about families on long drives where Mom rides in the back seat to keep the kids happy while Dad's alone in the front. We ask you, fellow baby boomers, can you visualize our parents doing that?

Schools hand out condoms with the underlying expectation that kids won't abstain from sex and that it will be unprotected sex, to boot. Children use birth control pills with their parents' blessing. Schools feel the need to provide "character" education or drug programs like D.A.R.E., Quest, and Boomerang. It's all about expectations. Low expectations.

If we want our children to get good grades, college scholarships, and good jobs with decent pay, while avoiding teenage pregnancy, drugs, sexually transmitted diseases, and all the other bad stuff, we'll need to have high expectations. But just having high expectations isn't enough. We'll also need to implement strategies to help our kids meet those expectations without driving them crazy. It's a matter of money, better lives, family harmony, and sometimes it's even a matter of life and death.

We're convinced that if we have high academic and behavioral expectations for our children, we'll have happier, healthier, more productive children *and* more peace and harmony at home. Happy, peaceful families spend less because they already feel good, just the way they are. There's a feeling of purpose, direction, fulfillment, and pride. There's a sense of mission: "This family is going to accomplish good things. We count!"

A recent study published in the *Journal of the American Medical Association* found that students who believed that their parents had high expectations of them were not as likely to suffer emotional distress, have suicidal thoughts and behaviors, or get into risk-taking behaviors like substance abuse.* So if you've bought into some of the pop psychology that would have parents asking little Suzie (in a sing-song voice) if maybe she'd like to go to bed now that it's 11:30 P.M., you might want to think again. It appears that kids with boundaries, kids whose parents expect them to succeed and behave, are doing better.

We decided early on, even before we had kids, that our most important mission as a couple was to raise children with good behavior and academic achievements consistent with their abilities. We believed that if we could achieve these two things with our kids, everything else would fall into place. Well-behaved children who are good students are happier, healthier, and more successful. We believe that. We care about behavior and academic achievement. It's how we measure our success or failure as parents. So when Colleen was bringing home mediocre grades in seventh grade and we felt she could do better, we gave her a choice:

1. Study 2 hours per night with no pressure from us to raise her grades, or
2. Get a 3.5 GPA with no pressure from us to study.

She choose the latter so fast it would make your head spin and we never saw less than a 3.5 GPA again. But if she hadn't been capable of earning a 3.5 GPA, making sure she studied regularly would have assured us she was doing her best.

---

*M. Resnick, Ph.D., et al., "Protecting Adolescents From Harm," *The Journal of the American Medical Association,* September 10, 1997, vol. 278, pp. 823–832.

But there's more to getting good grades than study. Most teachers offer opportunities to earn extra credit that can be used to supplement points lost on a botched test or assignment. We require our kids to take advantage of extra credit. Over the years it has turned several Bs into As, and besides, it's an easy way to eliminate pressure. It's a no-brainer. We require it.

Very rarely, we encounter a teacher who just isn't fair, and if we're convinced of that, we intervene. If the school grades on a four-point system (A through F) then it must be possible to get an A. If there are no students getting As, there might be a problem with the teacher.

Occasionally one of our children becomes overwhelmed with assignments, tests, part-time work, and extracurricular activities, but in our house that's viewed as an excellent opportunity to learn organizational skills. We all sit down and make a list and a schedule. If there's just too much to fit into a day, we'll pitch in and help. These simple assists usually provide a tremendous relief while also teaching organizational techniques.

If a child blows a test, there's a good chance they don't know the material, so we always ask if they grasp the concepts, especially in math. If they don't, we go over the material with them until they do. Sometimes all it takes is hearing and seeing it explained in a different way. But it's important to ask about each subject periodically to ensure that the child isn't missing some concepts that might be needed later.

Trying to survive in today's world with a high school education is like trying to live through January in Iowa in a tent. It's possible to do but you'd probably be miserable. So we celebrate high school graduation, but it's a celebration about growing up and leaving home—for college. Any child who is able will need postsecondary education so they won't end up working in a chicken processing plant. We've always talked about college, even when our kids were small, as if it were expected and the thought of quitting after high school has probably never entered their minds. If it did, we'd take them on a tour of a chicken plant.

What about behavioral expectations? We're believers in the power of peer pressure, so why not create an easy out in advance? Colleen was 14 or 15 and was visiting a friend in a town a few miles from home. At about 8:00 P.M., the parents left and boys arrived with beer. She wanted out. Fortunately, we had discussed this type of scenario and we were ready. She told her friend she wasn't feeling well (which was true, she was uncomfortable with the situation). I took her call and we proceeded through a prearranged script.

"Dad, I don't feel well."

"Are you telling me you want out of a situation?"

"Yes."

"Are you in any danger? It will take me 15 minutes to drive to you. Should I call the police?"

"No."

"Will you be safe for the 15 minutes it takes me to get there?"

"Yes."

"I'm on my way."

Colleen knew that she would be expected to bail out of situations like that. No excuses. But we had an obligation to make it as easy as possible for her to meet our expectations. We had a pact. We were in it together.

We're just average parents and often we feel that we don't know what we're doing. But we do know this: we care, we think, we try, we do our best. And we're convinced that one of the best things we can do for our children is to expect good things from them, to believe in them.

TEENS

Getting Through the Tough Years Without Losing Your Money or Your Mind

Your kids will become teens at about the same time that you'll be able to start packing away some serious bucks. The timing couldn't be worse. Troubles with teens can consume huge amounts of time, energy, and money. You'll want to approach teen problems like you deal with dreaded diseases. Prevention. An entire industry of psychologists and social workers exists to help parents deal with the demands of parenthood. Countless books have been written on the subject. Although you may not get around to using the parent education industry, you must make a plan for dealing with teen issues. Think about it, talk about it, and do what works for your family. Tackle these issues head on while your child is still young. One issue you'll face is your teen's need for freedom, which is at the root of most parent/adolescent conflicts. How will you deal with that?

Don't misunderstand, we're not pushing any specific parenting techniques here. What we are saying is this: If you want to accumulate significant assets fast, you can't be consumed by family problems or all you'll be able to do is slog through the day. Your mind will be occupied with fixing all the rifts. You'll toss and turn in bed but sleep soundly at work. We've all seen families with teen-related problems. It isn't a pretty sight. If you try to deal with these issues on the spur of the moment (like the first time Johnny still isn't home at 2:00 A.M.), you'll probably mess it up. So make a plan. Think it through. Develop a strategy that works for you.

Here's a glimpse of how our plan unfolded one night:

Dad: Colleen, you'll be a teenager soon and you need to know how we're going to do things.

Colleen: What do you mean?

Mom: We're going to do things differently than some of your friends' parents. There are going to be a lot of things that you'll want to do when you're a teenager and we're going to say "no."

Colleen: OK?? (Translation: "I don't like the sound of this!")

Dad: It's our job as parents to get you to adulthood but just getting you there isn't good enough. We want to get you there safely and we want you to be the best person you're capable of being. There's a lot of stuff you'll encounter as a teenager that is a threat to your safety and your character.

Colleen: What do you mean, "character"?

Mom: Your goodness or badness. It can go either way.

Dad: Right. So it is our job as parents to do everything we can to prevent injury to your body or your character. We take that job very seriously. Raising you is our number one priority right now and a sacred duty given to us by God. We must help you make it to adulthood safely and as a good person. Now, part of that is your responsibility, too, but as your mom and dad we've got to do all we can to keep you on the right track. Do you want that too?

Colleen: Yes, I do.

Dad: Good. So here's the deal. We won't let you hang out with kids that are trouble. If you choose a friend and we think that friend is a bum, we won't let you do things with that friend. You can choose any friends you want as long as they are good kids. That means we won't let you run with the "fast" crowd even though that may also be the most popular crowd. So you need to pick friends that are good, like you. If you don't, we'll clash but we won't back down because we can't. If we cave in, we'd be hurting you and we won't do that. No way. No how.

Colleen: OK.

Mom: Also, there will be times we won't let you do things your peers can do because we think it will harm you in some way. You won't like that but you need to know now so you're ready.

Colleen: I don't think that's fair.

Dad: You're right. It isn't fair and you won't like it but we are responsible for you and you are very important to us. We won't let ourselves fail in this. But Colleen, there's an upside to this too. Stuff you'll like.

Colleen: Like what?

Mom: We'll bend over backward to give you any freedom possible if it does no harm. We'll do that because we want to make your teenage years as easy as we can. We'll restrict your freedom only if we perceive potential harm to you. Otherwise we'll say "yes."

Colleen: I'm not sure I know what you mean.

Dad: Well, here's an example. You're how old now?

Colleen: Eleven.

Mom: And you've been asking about piercing your ears, right?

Colleen: Yes.

Dad: And we've said no because you're too young. Well, we were wrong. We've thought it through and we can't think of any harm that would come to you if you pierce your ears so you can do it, any time you want.

Colleen: Really?!?

Dad: Yes. From now on we'll give you any freedom that helps you save face with your friends and causes no harm.

Colleen: What's "save face?"

Mom: Not look like a nerd to your friends.

Dad: So we're in this together, Colleen. We're on your side . . . and you're on our side, right?

Colleen: Sure. Can I get my ears pierced tomorrow?

Colleen never gave us a bit of trouble. Meghann is 14 now and we've had the same discussion with her. So far she's been a complete delight. Hopefully she'll hold it together until long after we get this book published; otherwise we'll probably change our names and move to Canada or something. Hey, there are no guarantees!

AFTERWORD

The world, as always, is getting much better. Never in history have so many average families, like ours, had the opportunity to accumulate enough assets to make a real difference; enough to free us from full-time work while we're still relatively young. A combination of technological advancements and hard work have unleashed a level of productivity in this country that is unprecedented. But the benefits of all this productivity, as always, won't be distributed equitably between workers and managers/owners. So if you are average workers, like us, you'll probably work until the politicians say you can quit, unless you act.

If you don't like the idea of working full-time until you're 70 or 75, consider taking the path to financial freedom. If you're married, sit down with your spouse and have a heart-to-heart talk. Do it soon. Don't wait. Discuss your hopes, your fears, and your dreams. How do you want to spend the time that you have left together on this Earth? You may choose a traditional path and work until you can collect a pension and social security, and there's nothing wrong with that. If you enjoy your work and are content with your life, count your blessings. Maybe you'll choose a middle ground; pay off the mortgage early, save a hundred or two each month, and call it quits at 60 or 62. That would be a real accomplishment that many will never achieve. Perhaps you'll elect to reduce your spending and spend the money saved on things that will really improve the quality of your life or someone else's.

If, like us, you choose to put the pedal to the metal and achieve financial freedom in 8 or 10 years, keep three things in mind: protect your relationships no matter what the cost; control your spending, *not* your saving; and maintain an attitude of gratitude at all times. If you do these things, the rest will come.

As we write this, we're still working our regular jobs and that will probably continue for another year or two. Why? Well, we've decided that we want to live in a house on a lake, something we've always dreamed of, but never believed possible. And houses on the shores of lakes don't come cheap. But, you know, we really do enjoy our lives now, so another couple of years will be a breeze for us.

In closing, we're just average working people who set out to find a better way, and we hope our personal experiences will help you in some small way. Just remember, you don't need to change jobs, climb up the corporate ladder, or work in some high paying professional career to achieve financial freedom. Average people can do it too.

Good luck.

Index

Accountant, as information resource, 141
American Association of Individual
    Investors, 152
*American Association of Individual Investors
    Journal* (AAII Journal), 144, 152, 175
Annual expense ratio, 134
Appliances, buying guidelines, 86
Asset allocation
    defined, 171–172
    for low-risk investors, 176
    mutual funds, 178
    portfolio rebalancing, 188–189
    retirement plans and, 201–202
    strategies for, 172–175
Asset mix, 175
Association of State Medical Board
    Executive Directors, 87
Automatic bill paying services, 37
Automatic savings plans, 32–33
Automobile, *see* Cars

Bank fees, 86
Bank loans, for car, 61
Bank Rate Monitor, 86
Bankruptcy, 29, 44
Bank statements, 105
Bear market, 191, 215
Big ticket money savers
    cars, 59–66
    entertainment, 70–74
    grocery shopping, 67–69
    house, 55–58
    impulse buying and, 73–77

research, 83–87
scholarships, college education, 88–90
splurging and, 78–79
tax breaks, 91–95
Bogle, John, 148, 181
    on mutual fund investing, 150, 151
Bolles, Richard, 127
Bond investments
    asset allocation, 175–176
    benefits of, generally, 163–164
    corporate bonds, 166, 200
    defined, 164
    dividends, 166
    information resources, 152
    maturation, 166
    municipal bonds, 166, 183
    rating system, 165
    trading process, 164–165
Borrowing, 44–49. *See also specific types of
    loans*
Budgets, 29, 43
Bull market, 191
Bureau of Labor Statistics, 209
Business startups, 46

Canceled checks, 105
Capital gains, 160, 202
Cars
    buying tips, 59–66
    down payment, amount of, 60
    financing, 43
    insurance, 145
    loans, 46–47, 61

Cars (*cont.*)
  maintenance and repairs, 43, 62, 123–125, 126–127, 130–131
  new versus used, 62
  price negotiations, 65–66
  rustproofing option, 66
  sample maintenance record, 124
  used, information resources on, 65
Cash, investment versus, 168–170
Cashing in on the American Dream—How to Retire at 35 (Terhorst), 22
Certificates of deposit (CDs), 158, 166, 169, 173–174, 183, 200
Child-centered families, 227
College education expenses
  financial aid, 89, 99–100
  loans, 46
  public versus private colleges, 89–90
Comfort, in modest homes, 19–21
Commissions, 132–135
Common Sense in Mutual Funds: New Imperatives for the Intelligent Investor (Bogle), 148
Computers
  accounting software, 101
  do-it-yourself jobs, 128–129
necessity of, 100
Consumer complaints, guidelines for, 119–120
Consumer Price Index, 209
Consumer Reports, as information resource, 62, 86
Consumer research
  bank fees, 86
  computer hardware and software, 84–85
  importance of, generally, 87
  long-distance carriers, 85–86
  on major appliances, 86
  neighbors and friends as source for, 85
  physicians, 86–87
  schools and teachers, 85
Consumer World, 62, 86
Control issues, 14–15. *See also* Spending control
Coupon clipping, 68
Credit cards, 43, 45–47, 86, 173

Credit rating, 61
Credit union
  car loans from, 61
  savings account, 173
Crisis, maintaining normalcy during, 16–19

Debt, *See also specific types of debt*
  emotional impact of, 49
  paying off, 143
  Seven Steps to Eliminate Debt, 48
  types of, generally, 29, 44–49
Decorating tips, 20–21
Decorators, value of, 19–21, 79
Discipline, parenting tips for, 226–229
Discount brokerage, No Transaction Fee program, 192
Dividends, 159–160, 166, 202
Do-it-yourself jobs, as money savers, 126–131
Don't Miss Out: The Ambitious Student's Guide to Financial Aid (Leider/Leider), 89
Dow Jones Industrial Average, 180–181
Dr. Spock's Baby and Child Care (Spock), 128

Education, importance of, 143, 213–214, 233
Emergency cash reserve, 173, 199
Employment
  dependence on, 7
  downsizing and, 2
  problems with, 7
  purposes of, 5–6
Entertainment expenses
  couples only, 72
  family and kids, 71
Expectations, parental, 230–234
Expenses, types of, 40–43. *See also* Necessities

Family life
  dinners, 219–221
  entertainment ideas, 71
Fast food, 17, 220
Filing system, 103–106

Financial foundation, 142–145
Financial freedom, perspectives of, 5
Financial planners, 139–141
Financial planning, do-it-yourself, 127, 140–141
Food shopping, *see* Grocery shopping
457 plans, 200
401(k) plans, 46, 92, 188, 200
403(b) plans, 92, 200

Get a Financial Life: Personal Finance in Your Twenties and Thirties (Kobliner), 147
Gratitude, importance of, 25–27, 48, 75
Grocery shopping, 43, 67–68

Handbook for No-Load Investors, The (Jacobs), 147
Health care, information resource, 152, 213
Health insurance
  buying tips, 145
  coverage guidelines, 129–130, 213
  information resources, 213
Health maintenance organizations (HMOs), 130, 145
Heilbroner, Robert, 26–27
Hidden costs of living, types of, 41–42
"Holding" (Toohey), 224–225
Home(s)
  asset allocation and, 172–173
  buying tips, 55–58
  equity loans, 45–46
  financing, *see* Mortgages
  with one bathroom, 107–109
Household repairs, do-it-yourself jobs, 129
How to Want What You Have: Discovering the Magic and Grandeur of Ordinary Existence (Miller), 26, 147
How to Be Your Own Doctor (Sometimes) (Sehnert), 128

Ibbotson Associates, 148
Impulse buying, 73–77
Impulse Buying Processor, 76–77
Indexes, 180–181

Index funds, 181–182, 184, 189
Individual retirement accounts (IRAs), 92, 173, 188, 201, 205
Inflation
  cash and, 169
  retirement plan investments and, 207–210
  stock investments and, 162
Insurance
  amount of, 144–145
  car, 145
  cash value, 134
  disability, 144
  financial products, sales commissions on, 132–135
  health, 129–130, 145
  life, 134, 144
  long-term care, 214
  types of, generally, 134
Interest rates
  bond market and, 165
  on car loans, 46–47, 61
  on credit cards, 47
  on home equity loans, 45
Interior decorating, 19–21
Internal Revenue Service, 92, 198, 205
  publications, as information resource, 198
Internet, as information resource, 62–63, 66, 84–85, 128–129, 149–152
Investment(s)
  asset allocation, 171–177, 193
  bonds, 163–167
  broker, 140
  buy/sell strategies, 188–189
  cash versus, 168–170
  dollar-cost averaging, 187, 189
  indexes and, 180–181
  information resources, 146–153
  long-term, 160–162
  lump sum investing, 188
  mindset, 193
  mistakes, 190–193
  mutual funds, 93, 105, 133–134, 177–179
  portfolio diversification, 169–170
  risk, 169

Investment(s) (*cont.*)
  selection factors, 180–185
  stocks, 157–162
  taxation, 191–192
  threats to, generally, 212–215
  timing of, 185–189

Jacobs, Sheldon, 147
Job loss, planning for, 143
Job placement/resume services, do-it-yourself, 127
Journal of the American Medical Association, 232

Katter, Peter C., 144
Keeping up with the Joneses, 14, 25
Kennedy/Kassebaum legislation, 130, 213
Kids' entertainment ideas, 71
Killer of Love list, 14–15
Kiplinger, 152
Knock 'Em Dead (Yate), 127
Kobliner, Beth, 147

Lawyers Weekly USA, 201
Leider, Anna J. and Robert, 89
Lifestyle, simplicity in, 13–14
Liquidity, 178
Living More with Less (Longacre), 148
Longacre, Doris, 148

Magazines, as information resource, 149–150
Maintenance and repairs, benefits of, 122–125
Managed health care, 145
Market timers, 191
Market timing, 186–187
Meals
  family dinners, 219–221
  home-cooked, 17
  restaurant, 72, 78
Medical care, do-it-yourself, 127–128
Medical records, disputes with, 120–121
Medicare, 210, 214
Miller, Timothy, 26, 147
Money Magazine, 3–4, 152
Money management, professional, 7

Money-saving mindset, components of
  comfort, in modest homes, 19–21, 58
  crisis, maintaining normalcy during, 16–19
  gratitude, importance of, 25–27
  love, impact of money on relationships, 13–15, 240
  study, learning contributes to peace, order and financial freedom, 22–24
Moody's, 165
Mortgages
  accelerated payments, 57
  interest on, 46, 56–57
  paying off, 200–201
  tax deductions, 91–92
Municipal bonds, 166, 183
Mutual funds
  beneficiary, 179
  fees, 133–134, 178–179, 182, 191
  index funds, 181–182, 184, 189
  no-load funds, 134, 177–179, 192
  No Transaction Fee (NTF) programs, 192–193
  prospectus, 105, 179
  retirement plans, 202–203
  selection factors, 180–184, 191
  statement, 105
  taxation, 93
Myers, David, 6

Necessities
  cars, 59–66
  entertainment, 70–74
  grocery shopping, 67–69
  house, 55–58
  impulse buying and, 73–77
  overview, 52
  splurging and, 78–79
Needs, reduction in, 35
Net worth statement, 172
No-load funds, 134, 177–179, 192
No Transaction Fee (NTF) program, 192–193

Office supplies, 99–102
Overworked American: The Unexpected Decline of Leisure, The (Schor), 2, 148

Parenting issues
  bed time rituals, 111
  discipline, 226–229
  expectations, 230–234
  family dinners, 219–221
  indulgence, 222–225
  medical care, 128
  nightmares, dealing with, 112
  sleeping late, 112–113
  sick children, 112
  teenagers, 235–238
Passbook savings accounts, 173
"Pay yourself first" philosophy, 31
Personal Finance for Dummies (Tyson), 147
Physicians, selection factors, 86–87
PK Communications, 85
Plain Talk series, on Internet, 150, 151,
  167
Portfolio
  diversification, 170
  rebalancing, 188–189
Poverty, 26
Practical money-saving skills
  do-it-yourself jobs, 126–131
  maintenance, 122–125
  refunds, 117–121
  sales commissions, 132–135, 140
Price Watch, 84
Printer, necessity of, 100
Professional associations, as information
  resource, 152
Prospectus, 105, 179

Quicken, 101

*Reader's Digest New Complete Do-It-
  Yourself Manual*, 129
Reading, importance of, 23–24
Real return, 169
Record keeping
  bank statements, 105
  canceled checks, 105
  refunds and, 119. *See also* Filing system
Refunds
  dispute resolution guidelines, 119–121
  examples of, 117–119
Reichenstein, William, 175

Relationships, impact of money on,
  13–15, 240
Resumes, 127
Retirement plans
  accessibility issues, 199–200
  amount of investment, 207–211
  flaws of, 197–198
  lockup, 197, 199, 202
  mutual funds, 202
  periodic payments, 199–200, 205
  specialists, 200
  taxation, generally, 92–93, 198–199
  withdrawals, 204–206, 209–210, 215
Roth IRA, 201, 206

St. James, Elaine, 147
Savings plans, 31–33
Scholarships, for college education,
  88–90
School activities, importance of, 78
Schor, Juliet B., 2, 148
Scott, David Logan, 148–149
Sehnert, Keith W., 128
Select Quote, life insurance search
  service, 144
SEPs, 92, 200
Seven Steps to Eliminate Debt, 48
Sharpe, William, 175
Siegel, Jeremy J., 147, 160, 169
Silverman, David, 92, 147–148
SIMPLE IRAs, 92, 198, 200
Simplifying life, strategies for
  filing system, 103–106
  office supplies, 99–102
  one bathroom homes, 107–109
  sleep distractions, 110–113
*Simplify Your Life: 100 Ways to Slow Down
  and Enjoy the Things That Really
  Matter* (St. James), 147
Sleep distractions, 110–113
Social Security, 45, 210, 214
Social Security Administration, 56
Social Security Disability Insurance, 144
Social Security Trust Fund, 214
Spending control, 34–35, 73–77, 78
Spending habits, tracking system for,
  37–39

Spending less strategies
  borrowing and, 44–49
  categorize spending, 36–39
  saving, 31–33
  spending control, 34–35, 73–77, 78
  standard of living increases, 50–52
  surprise expenses, 40–43
Spending rate, 208
Splurging, 78–79
Spock, Benjamin, 128
Standard of living, 35, 50–52
Standard & Poor's (S&P) 500, 180–181
Stationery supplies, 101
Stock investments
  asset allocation, 175–176
  capital gain, 160
  dividends, 159–160, 202
  long-term, 160–162
  retirement plans, 201
  risks, 169
*Stocks, Bonds, Bills, and Inflation: 1998
  Yearbook* (Ibbotson Associates), 148
*Stocks for the Long Run: The Definitive
  Guide to Financial Market Returns and
  Long-Term Investment Strategies*
  (Siegel), 147, 160, 169
Study, benefits of, 22–24
Substantial equal periodic payments,
  retirement plan withdrawals, 205
Sworsky, Edgar, 86

Taxation
  benefits of, 95
  investments and, 191–192
  mutual funds, 93
  refunds, 94
  retirement accounts, 93–94, 198–199,
    201–202, 204
  standard deductions, 92
  tax brackets, 94, 183
Tax brackets, 94, 183
Tax breaks, 91–95
Tax returns
  do-it-yourself, 127
  Kiplinger TaxCut (Block Financial)
    computer program, 92

TurboTax (Intuit) computer program,
  92
Taxes for Dummies (Tyson/Silverman),
  92, 147–148
Teenagers, tips for dealing with,
  235–238
Telephone services
  long-distance carriers, 85–86
  slamming, 86
Terhorst, Paul, 22–23
Timing, of investments, 185–189
Toohey, Rosemary, 224
Treasury Inflation-Inflated Securities,
  167, 183–184
Tyson, Eric, 92, 147–148

U.S. Treasury, "Treasury Direct," 184
U.S. Treasury Bills, 169
U.S. Treasury Bonds, 183
USAA, 140, 183, 200

Vanguard Financial Group, 140, 163, 200
  funds, 181–183, 193
  Plain Talk series, 150, 151, 167
Volatility, stock investments and, 162,
  164

*Wall Street Words: An Essential A to Z
  Guide for Today's Investor* (Scott),
  148–149
Well-being, 21, 137, 140
What Color Is Your Parachute? (Bolles),
  127
Withdrawals, from retirement plans,
  204–206, 209–210, 215
Work, *see* Employment
Workforce Development and Job
  Training Partnership Act (JTPA),
  213–214
Workplace, benefits of, 5–6

Yate, Martin, 127

ZD Net, 84
Zweig, Jason, 152